PYTHON MACHINE LEARNING
WORKBOOK FOR BEGINNERS

10 MACHINE LEARNING PROJECTS
EXPLAINED FROM SCRATCH

AI PUBLISHING

First Printing, 2020

Edited by AI Publishing
eBook Converted and Cover by Gazler Studio
Published by AI Publishing LLC

ISBN-13: 978-1-7347901-7-7

How to Contact Us

If you have any feedback, please let us know
by sending an email to contact@aipublishing.io.

Your feedback is immensely valued,
and we look forward to hearing from you.
It will be beneficial for us
to improve the quality of our books.

To get the Python codes and materials used in this book,
please click the link below:

www.aipublishing.io/book-mlworkbook-python

The order number is required.

About the Publisher

At AI Publishing Company, we have established an international learning platform specifically for young students, beginners, small enterprises, startups, and managers who are new to data science and artificial intelligence.

Through our interactive, coherent, and practical books and courses, we help beginners learn skills that are crucial to developing AI and data science projects.

Our courses and books range from basic introduction courses to language programming and data science to advanced courses for machine learning, deep learning, computer vision, big data, and much more. The programming languages used include Python, R, and some data science and AI software.

AI Publishing's core focus is to enable our learners to create and try proactive solutions for digital problems by leveraging the power of AI and data science to the maximum extent.

Moreover, we offer specialized assistance in the form of our online content and eBooks, providing up-to-date and useful insight into AI practices and data science subjects, along with eliminating the doubts and misconceptions about AI and programming.

Our experts have cautiously developed our contents and kept them concise, short, and comprehensive so that you can understand everything clearly and effectively and start practicing the applications right away.

We also offer consultancy and corporate training in AI and data science for enterprises so that their staff can navigate through the workflow efficiently.

With AI Publishing, you can always stay closer to the innovative world of AI and data science.

If you are eager to learn the A to Z of AI and data science but have no clue where to start, AI Publishing is the finest place to go.

Please contact us by email at
contact@aipublishing.io.

AI Publishing is Looking for Authors Like You

Interested in becoming an author for AI Publishing? Please contact us at author@aipublishing.io.

We are working with developers and AI tech professionals just like you, to help them share their insights with the global AI and Data Science lovers. You can share all your knowledge about hot topics in AI and Data Science.

Table of Contents

Preface

Thank you for your decision to purchase this book. I can assure you that you will not regret your decision. The term *data is the new oil* is no longer a mere cliché. Data is actually powering the industries of today. Organizations and companies need to improve their growth, which depends upon correct decision-making. Accurate decision-making requires facts, figures, and statistical analysis of data, leading to the identification of important data patterns. Data science does exactly that. With data and machine learning, you can extract and visualize data in detail and create statistical models, which, in turn, help you in decision-making. In this book, you will learn all these concepts. So, buckle up for a journey that may give you your career break!

§ Book Approach

The book follows a very simple approach. It is divided into two sections.

The first section consists of two chapters. Chapter 1 presents a very concise introduction to data science and machine learning and provides a roadmap for step by step learning approach to data science and machine learning. The process for environment setup, including the software needed to run scripts in this book, is also explained in this chapter. Chapter 2 contains a crash course on Python for beginners. If you are already familiar with Python, you can skip chapter 2.

The second section consists of 10 interesting machine learning and data science-based projects.

Project 1 shows how you can predict the sale price of a house using linear regression. Successful completion of this project will help you apply the knowledge you gain to solve any supervised regression problem.

In the 2nd project, you will be developing a ham and spam message classifier using naïve Bayes algorithm. The concepts explained in this project can be transferred to any text classification task.

The third project introduces you to the world of artificial neural networks, where you use a densely connected neural network to predict car sale prices. The concepts you learn in this project are essential to solve any regression problem via artificial neural networks.

In project 4, you will study how to predict stock market trends using LSTM, which is a type of recurrent neural network. Successful completion of this project will help you in tackling time series problems via the LSTM.

The 5th project explains the process of language translation using sequence to sequence LSTM. With the sequence to sequence LSTM, you can solve pretty much any problem where inputs and outputs both are sequences of data.

In project 6, you will study how you can classify dog and cat images using a convolutional neural network (CNN). The concepts learned in this project are applicable to any image classification task.

The 7th project shows how you can create a movie recommender system based on the correlation between movie features. The ideas explained in this project are applicable to any other recommender system, as well.

In project 8, you will perform a very interesting task of detecting faces from images. You will see how to recognize human faces, eyes, and smiles from images and videos.

The 9th project explains how you can recognize handwritten English alphabets with a convolutional neural network. This project is comparable to project 6, but instead of binary classification, in this project, you will see how to perform multiclass classification on the image data.

Finally, in the 10th and last project, you will create a customer segmentation model based on the K-means clustering algorithm that segments customers into groups based on their income and spending habits. The concepts you learn in this project can be used to model any clustering system.

In each project, a brief explanation of the theoretical concepts is given, followed by practical examples. The Python notebook for each project is provided in the *Source Codes* folder in GitHub and SharePoint repositories. It is advised that instead of copying the code, you write the code yourself, and in case of an error, you match your code with the corresponding Python notebook, find and then correct the error. The datasets used in this book are easily accessible. You can either download them at runtime or they are available in the *Datasets* folder in the GitHub and SharePoint repositories.

§ Who Is This Book For?

This book contains hands-on data science and machine learning concepts. The book is aimed ideally at absolute beginners to data science and machine learning. The idea is to allow students to quickly build a working tool instead of getting lost in the labyrinths of complex mathematics.

The concepts are explained at a high level without digging deeper into the mathematical details. In addition, though a background in the Python programming language and feature engineering can help speed up learning, the book contains a crash course on Python programming language in the first chapter. Therefore, the only prerequisites to efficiently using this book are access to a computer with the internet and basic knowledge of linear algebra and calculus. All the codes and datasets have been provided. However, to download data preparation libraries, you will need the internet.

§ How to Use This Book?

To get the best out of this book, I would suggest that you first get your feet wet with the Python programming language, especially the object-oriented programming concepts. To do so, you can take the crash course on Python in chapter 2 of this book. Also, try to complete the projects in this book in order since, in some cases, the concepts taught in subsequent projects are based on previous projects.

In each project, try to first understand the theoretical concepts behind different types of data science and machine learning techniques and then try to execute the example code. I would again stress that rather than copying and pasting code, try to write codes yourself, and in case of any error, you can match your code with the source code provided in the book, as well as in the Python notebooks in the Source Codes folder in GitHub. Finally, try to answer the questions asked in the exercises at the end of each project. The solutions to the exercises have been given at the end of the book.

To facilitate the reading process, occasionally, the book presents three types of box-tags in different colors: **Requirements**, **Further Readings,** and **Hands-on Time**. Examples of these boxes are shown below.

Requirements
This box lists all requirements needed to be done before proceeding to the next topic. Generally, it works as a checklist to see if everything is ready before a tutorial.

Further Readings
Here, you will be pointed to some external reference or source that will serve as additional content about the specific **Topic** being studied. In general, it consists of packages, documentations, and cheat sheets.

Hands-on Time
Here, you will be pointed to an external file to train and test all the knowledge acquired about a **Tool** that has been studied. Generally, these files are Jupyter notebooks (.ipynb), Python (.py) files, or documents (.pdf).

The box-tag **Requirements** lists the steps required by the reader after reading one or more topics. **Further Readings** provides relevant references for specific topics to get to know the additional content of the topics. **Hands-on Time** points to practical tools to start working on the specified topics. Follow the instructions given in the box-tags to get a better understanding of the topics presented in this book.

About the Author

M. Usman Malik holds a Ph.D. in Computer Science from Normandy University, France, with Artificial Intelligence and Machine Learning being his main areas of research. Muhammad Usman Malik has over 5 years of industry experience in Data Science and has worked with both private and public sector organizations. In his free time, he likes to listen to music and play snooker.

Get in Touch With Us

Feedback from our readers is always welcome.

For general feedback, please send us an email at contact@aipublishing.io and mention the book title in the subject line.

Although we have taken extraordinary care to ensure the accuracy of our content, errors do occur. If you have found an error in this book, we would be grateful if you could report this to us as soon as you can.

If you are interested in becoming an AI Publishing author and if you have expertise in a topic and you are interested in either writing or contributing to a book, please send us an email at author@aipublishing.io.

An Important Note to Our Valued Readers:

Download the Color Images

Our print edition books are available only in black & white at present. However, the digital edition of our books is available in color PDF.

We request you to download the PDF file containing the color images of the screenshots/diagrams used in this book here:

www.aipublishing.io/book-mlworkbook-python

The typesetting and publishing costs for a color edition are prohibitive. These costs would push the final price of each book to $50, which would make the book less accessible for most beginners.

We are a small company, and we are negotiating with major publishers for a reduction in the publishing price. We are hopeful of a positive outcome sometime soon. In the meantime, we request you to help us with your wholehearted support, feedback, and review.

For the present, we have decided to print all of our books in black & white and provide access to the color version in PDF. This is a decision that would benefit the majority of our readers, as most of them are students. This would also allow beginners to afford our books.

Warning

In Python, indentation is very important. Python indentation is a way of telling a Python interpreter that the group of statements belongs to a particular code block. After each loop or if-condition, be sure to pay close attention to the intent.

Example

```
# Python program showing
# indentation

site = 'aisciences'

if site == 'aisciences':
    print('Logging to www.aisciences.io...')
else:
    print('retype the URL.')
print('All set !')
```

To avoid problems during execution, we advise you to download the codes available on Github by requesting access from the link below. Please have your order number ready for access:

www.aipublishing.io/book-mlworkbook-python

CHAPTER

1

Introduction and Environment Set Up

Data science libraries exist in various programming languages. However, you will be using Python programming language for data science and machine learning since Python is flexible, easy to learn, and offers the most advanced data science and machine learning libraries. Furthermore, Python has a huge data science community from where you can take help whenever you want.

In this chapter, you will see how to set up the Python environment needed to run various data science and machine learning libraries. The chapter also contains a crash Python course for absolute beginners to Python. Finally, the different data science and machine learning libraries that we are going to study in this book have been discussed. The chapter ends with a simple exercise.

1.1. Difference between Data Science and Machine Learning?

The terms data science and machine learning are often interchangeably used. However, the two terms are different. Data science is a sphere of study that uses scientific approaches and mathematical techniques such as statistics to draw out meaning and insights from data. As per Dr. Thomas Miller from Northwestern University, data science is "a combination of information technology, modeling and business management."

Machine learning, on the other hand, is an approach consisting of mathematical algorithms that enable computers to make decisions without being explicitly performed. Rather, machine learning algorithms learn from data, and then, based on the insights from the dataset, they make decisions without human input.

In this book, you will complete projects that involve both data science and machine learning since you will be importing datasets, analyzing them, and finally, implementing machine learning models with them.

1.2. Steps in Learning Data Science and Machine Learning

1. Know What Data Science and Machine Learning Is All About

Before you delve deep into developing data science and machine learning applications, you have to know what the field of data science and machine learning is, what you can do with that, and what are some of the best tools and libraries that you can use.

2. Learn a Programming Language

If you wish to be a data science and machine learning expert, you have to learn programming. There is no working around this fact. Although there are several cloud-based machine learning platforms like Amazon Sage Maker and Azure ML Studio where you can create data science applications without writing a single line of code, however, to get fine-grained control over your applications, you will need to learn programming.

Though you can program natural language applications in any programming language, I would recommend that you learn Python programming language. Python is one of the most commonly used libraries for data science and machine learning, with myriads of basic and advanced data science and ML libraries. In addition, many data science applications are based on deep learning and machine learning techniques. Again, Python is the language that provides easy to use libraries for deep learning and machine learning.

3. Start with the Basics

Start with very basic data science applications. I would rather recommend that you should not start developing data science applications right away. Start with basic mathematical and numerical operations like computing dot products and matrix multiplication, etc.

4. Learn Machine Learning and Deep Learning Algorithms

Data Science, machine learning, and deep learning go hand to hand. Therefore, you have to learn machine learning and deep learning algorithms. In machine learning, start with the supervised learning techniques. Supervised machine learning algorithms are divided into two types, i.e., regression and classification.

5. Develop Data Science Applications

Once you are familiar with basic machine learning and deep learning algorithms, you are good to go for developing data science applications. Data science applications can be of different types, i.e., predicting house prices, recognizing images, classifying text, etc. Being a beginner, you should try to develop versatile data science applications, and later, when you find your area of interest, e.g., natural language processing or image recognition, delve deep into that. It is important to mention that this book provides a very generic introduction to data science, and you will see applications of data science to structured data, textual data, and image data. However, this book is not dedicated to any specific data science field.

6. Deploying Data Science Applications

To put a data science or machine learning application into production so that anyone can use it, you need to deploy it to production. There are several ways to deploy data science applications. You can use dedicated servers containing REST APIs that can be used to call various functionalities in your data science application. To deploy such applications, you need to learn Python Flask, Docker, or similar web technology. In addition to that, you can also deploy your applications using Amazon Web Services or any other cloud-based deployment platform.

To be an expert data science and machine learning practitioner, you need to perform the aforementioned six steps in an iterative manner.

1.3. Environment Setup

1.3.1. Windows Setup

The time has come to install Python on Windows using an IDE. In fact, we will use Anaconda throughout this book, right from installing Python to writing multi-threaded codes in the coming lectures. Now, let us get going with the installation.

This section explains how you can download and install Anaconda on Windows.

Follow these steps to download and install Anaconda.

1. Open the following URL in your browser.

   https://www.anaconda.com/distribution/

2. The browser will take you to the following webpage. Select the latest version of Python (3.7 at the time of writing this book). Now, click the *Download* button to download the executable file. Depending upon the speed of your internet, the file will download within 2–3 minutes.

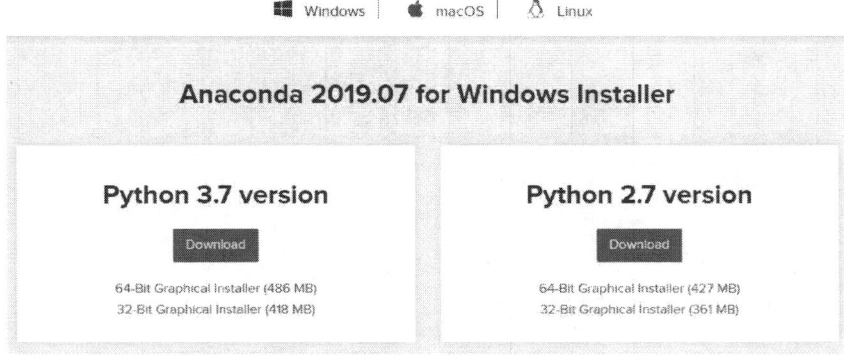

3. Run the executable file after the download is complete. You will most likely find the download file in your download folder. The name of the file should be similar to "Anaconda3-

5.1.0-Windows-x86_64." The installation wizard will open when you run the file, as shown in the following figure. Click the *Next* button.

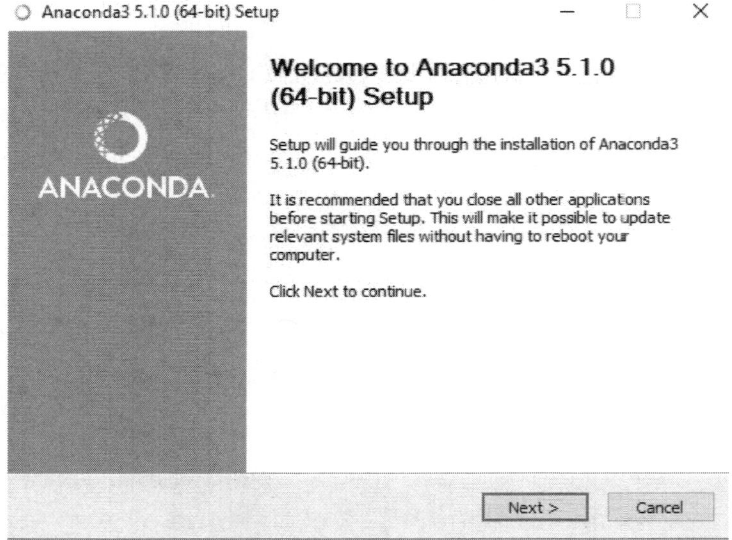

4. Now click *I Agree* on the *License Agreement* dialog as shown in the following screenshot.

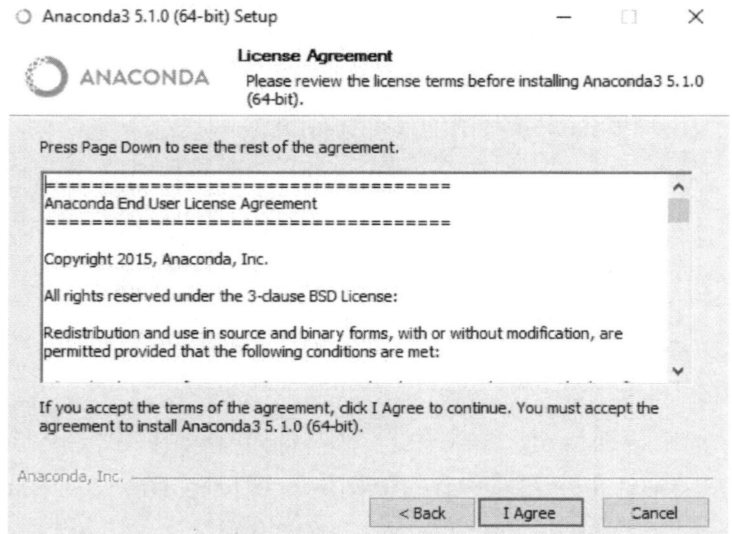

5. Check the *Just Me* radio button from the *Select Installation Type* dialogue box. Click the *Next* button to continue.

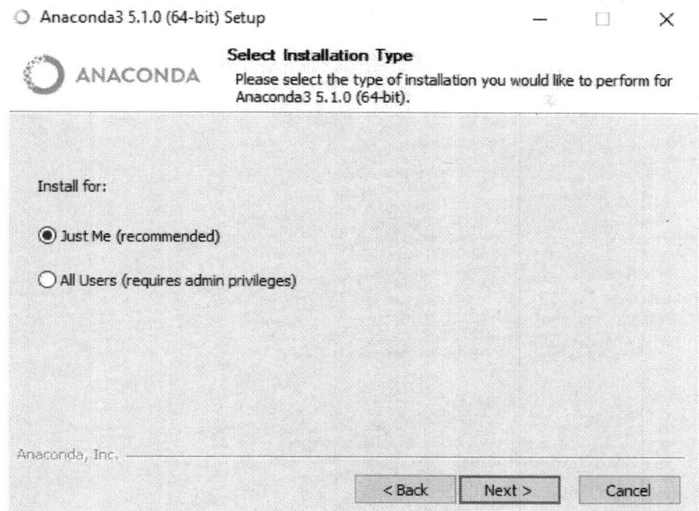

6. Now, the *Choose Install Location* dialog will be displayed. Change the directory if you want, but the default is preferred. The installation folder should at least have 3 GB of free space for Anaconda. Click the *Next* button.

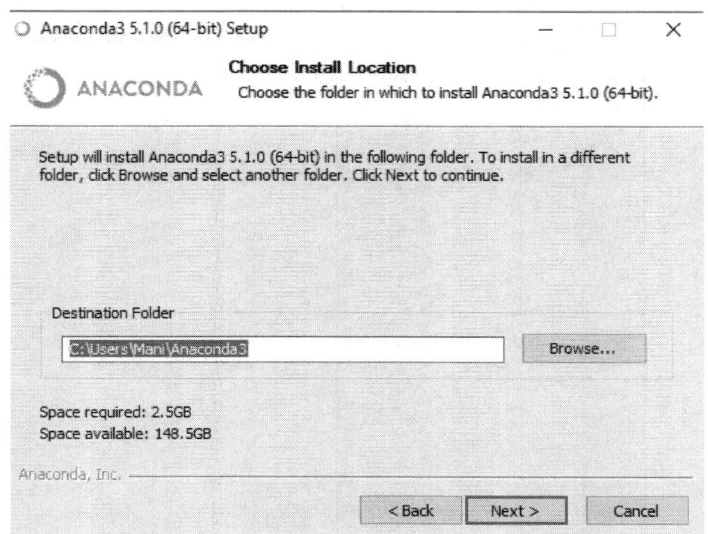

7. Go for the second option, *Register Anaconda as my default Python 3.7* in the *Advanced Installation Options* dialog box. Click the *Install* button to start the installation, which can take some time to complete.

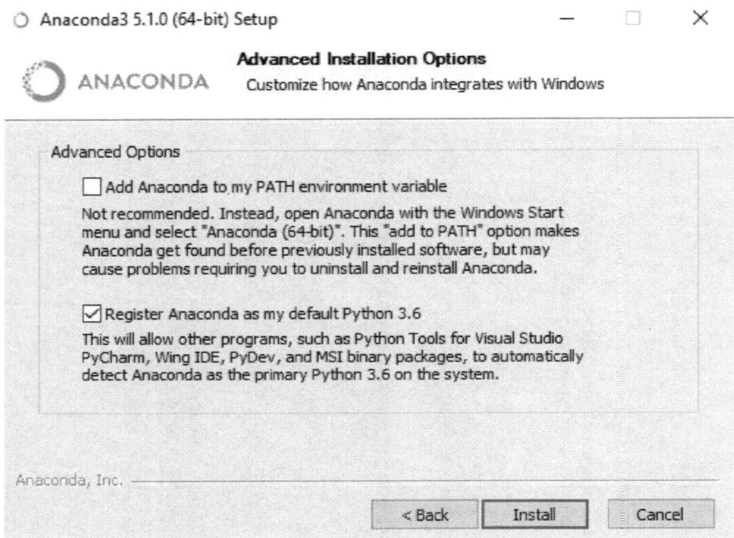

8. Click *Next* once the installation is complete.

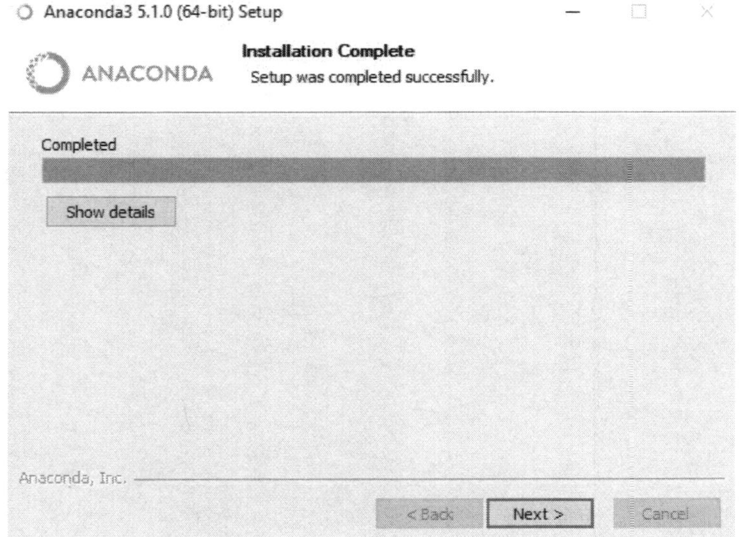

9. Click *Skip* on the *Microsoft Visual Studio Code Installation* dialog box.

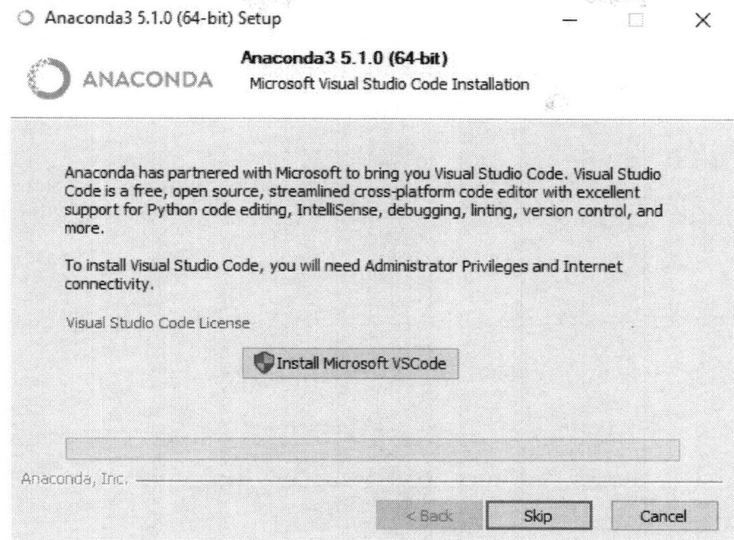

10. You have successfully installed Anaconda on your Windows. Excellent job. The next step is to uncheck both checkboxes on the dialog box. Now, click on the *Finish* button.

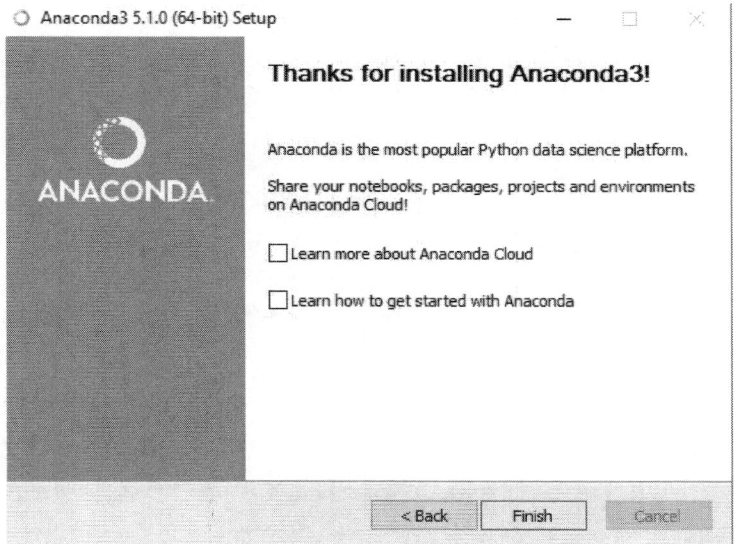

1.3.2. Mac Setup

Anaconda's installation process is almost the same for Mac. It may differ graphically, but you will follow the same steps you followed for Windows. The only difference is that you have to download the executable file, which is compatible with the Mac operating system.

This section explains how you can download and install Anaconda on Mac.

Follow these steps to download and install Anaconda.

1. Open the following URL in your browser.

   https://www.anaconda.com/distribution/

2. The browser will take you to the following webpage. Select the latest version of Python for Mac. (3.7 at the time of writing this book). Now, click the *Download* button to download the executable file. Depending upon the speed of your internet, the file will download within 2–3 minutes.

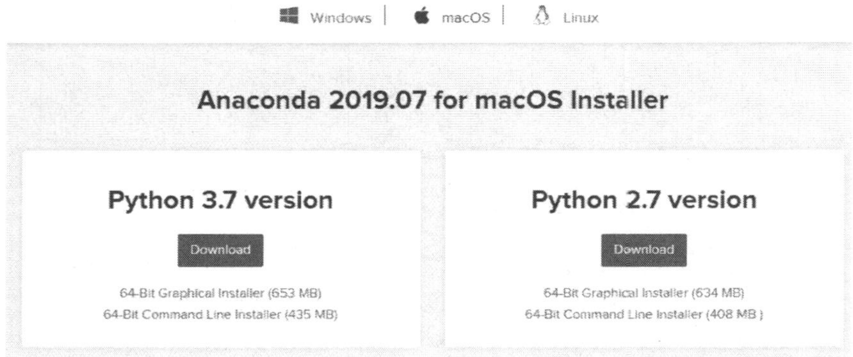

3. Run the executable file after the download is complete. You will most likely find the download file in your download folder. The name of the file should be similar to "Anaconda3-5.1.0-Windows-x86_64." The installation wizard will open

when you run the file, as shown in the following figure. Click the *Continue* button.

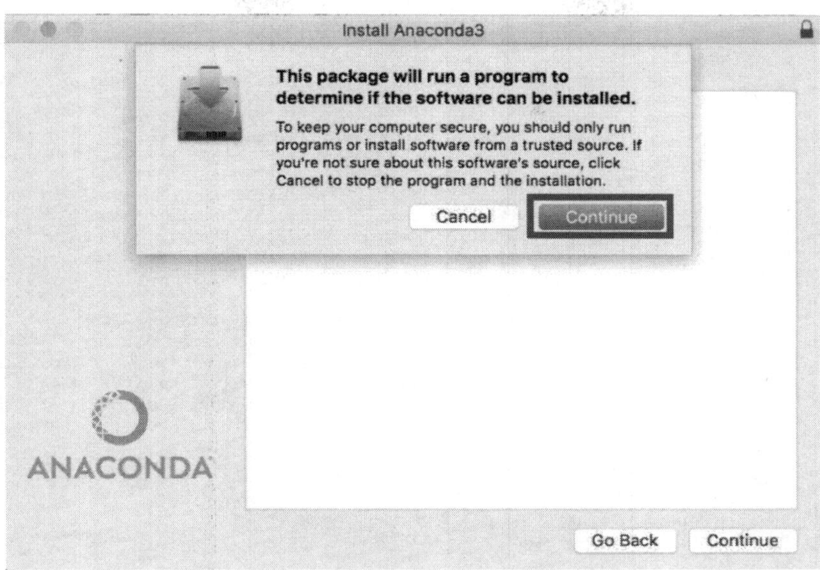

4. Now, click, *Continue* on the *Welcome to Anaconda 3 Installer* window, as shown in the following screenshot.

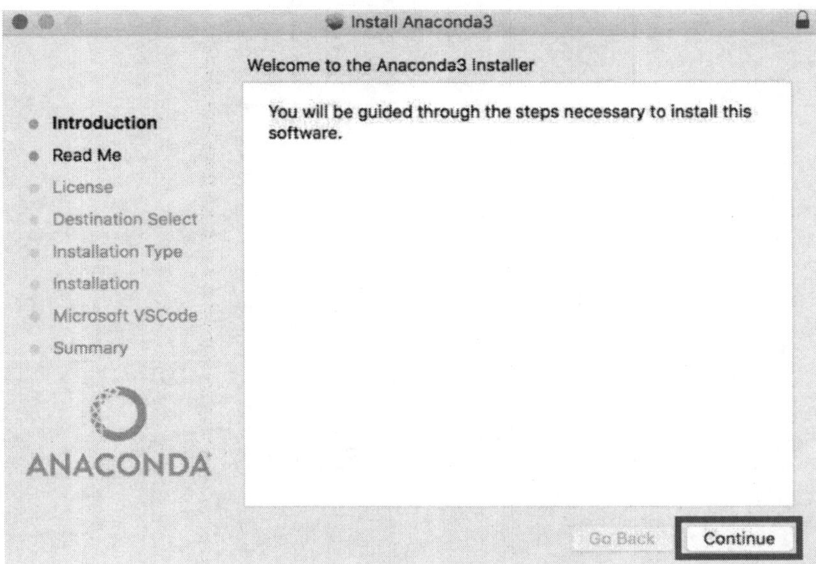

5. The *Important Information* dialog will pop up. Simply click *Continue* to go with the default version that is Anaconda 3.

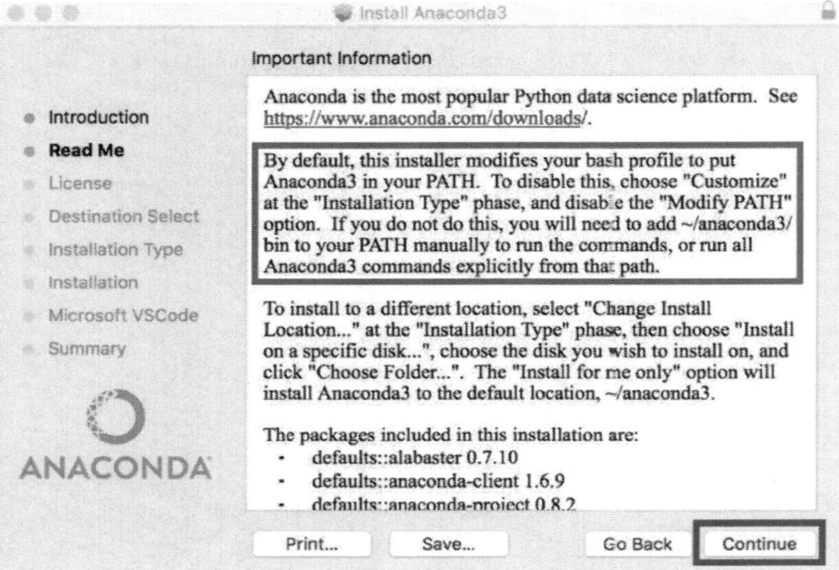

6. Click *Continue* on the *Software License Agreement* Dialog.

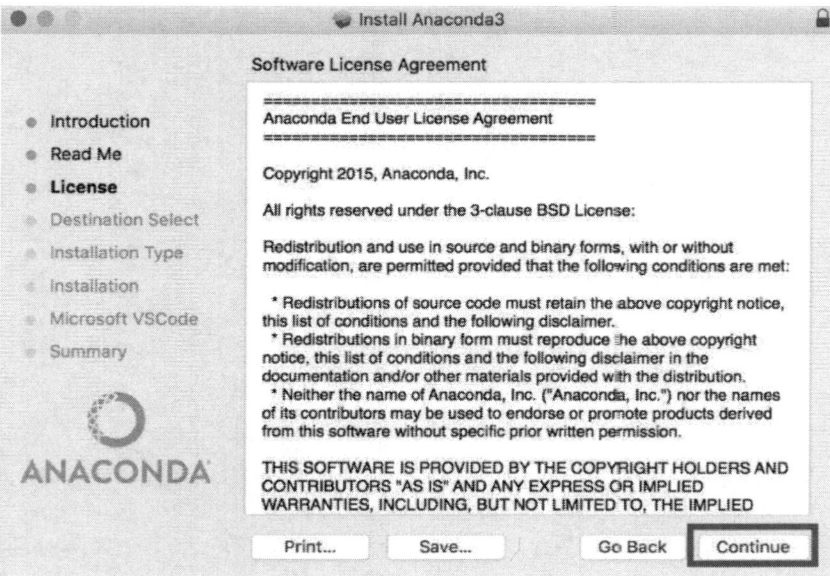

7. It is mandatory to read the license agreement and click the *Agree* button before you can click the *Continue* button again.

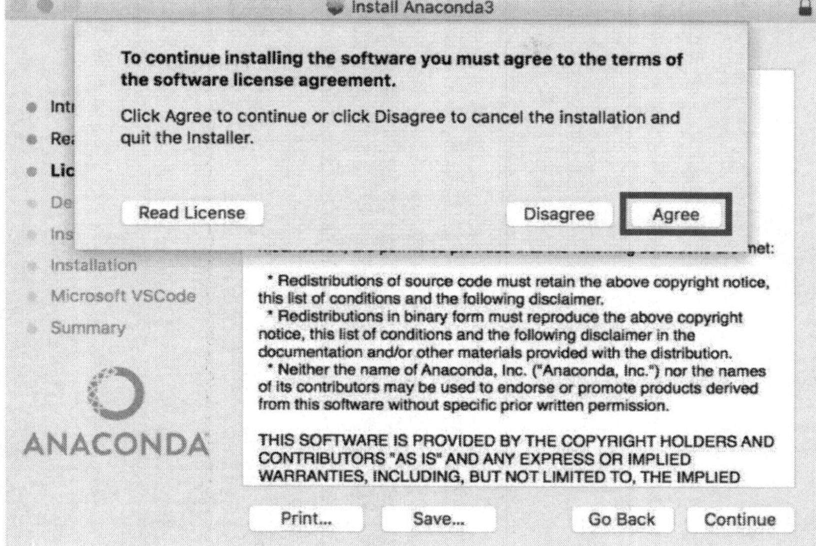

8. Simply click *Install* on the next window that appears.

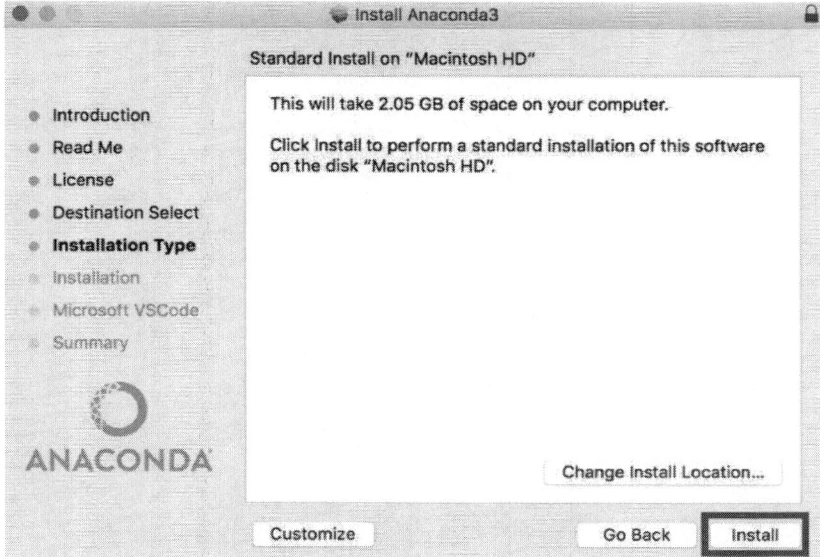

The system will prompt you to give your password. Use the same password you use to login to your Mac computer. Now, click on *Install Software*.

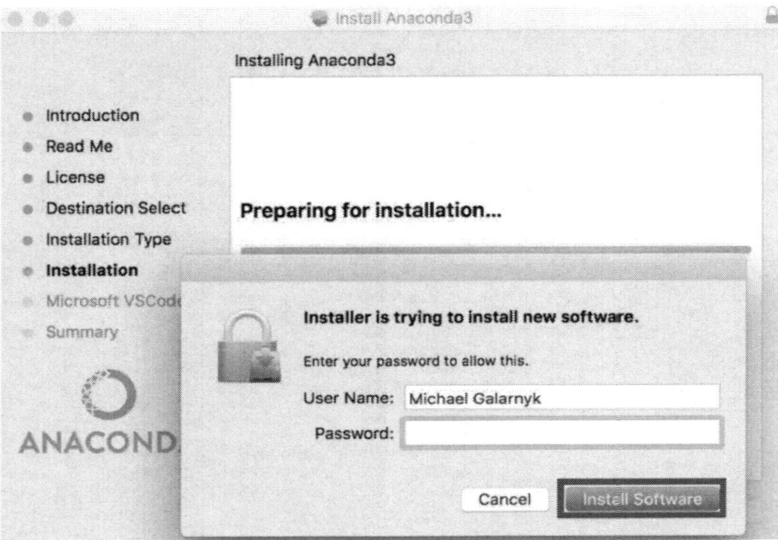

9. Click *Continue* on the next window. You also have the option to install Microsoft VSCode at this point.

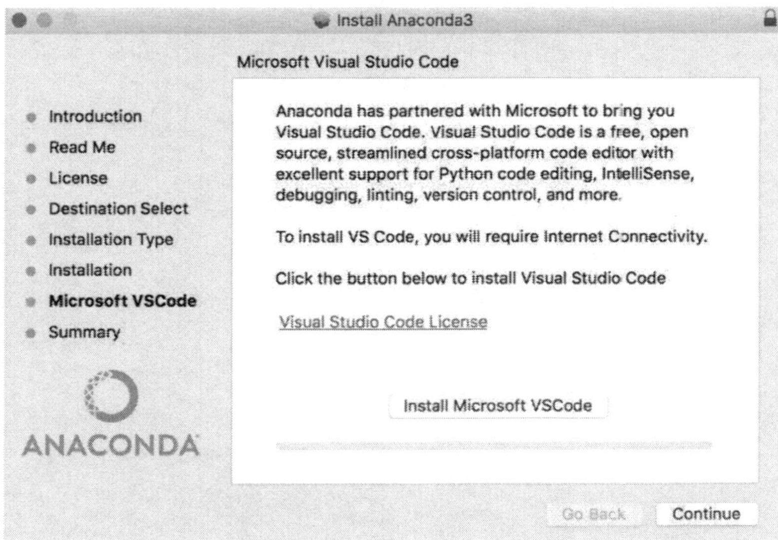

The next screen will display the message that the installation has been completed successfully. Click on the *Close* button to close the installer.

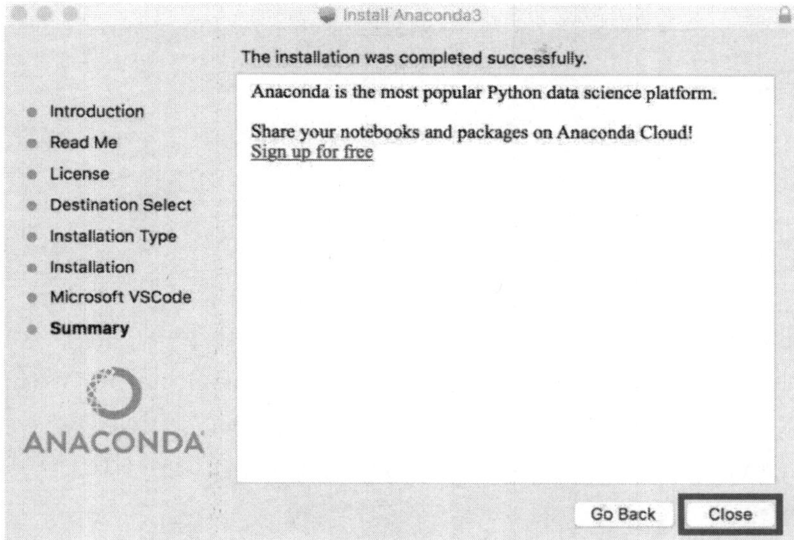

There you have it. You have successfully installed Anaconda on your Mac computer. Now, you can write Python code in Jupyter and Spyder the same way you wrote it in Windows.

1.3.3. Linux Setup

We have used Python's graphical installers for installation on Windows and Mac. However, we will use the command line to install Python on Ubuntu or Linux. Linux is also more resource-friendly, and the installation of software is particularly easy as well.

Follow these steps to install Anaconda on Linux (Ubuntu distribution).

1. Go to the following link to copy the installer bash script from the latest available version.

https://www.anaconda.com/distribution/

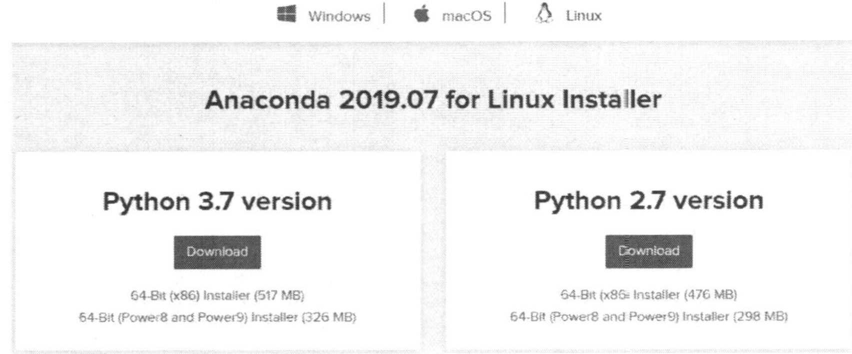

2. The second step is to download the installer bash script. Log into your Linux computer and open your terminal. Now, go to /temp directory and download the bash you downloaded from Anaconda's home page using curl.

```
$ cd / tmp

$ curl -o https://repo.anaconda.com.archive/Anaconda3-
5.2.0-Linux-x86_64.sh
```

3. You should also use the cryptographic hash verification through the SHA-256 checksum to verify the integrity of the installer.

```
$ sha256sum Anaconda3-5.2.0-Linux-x86_64.sh
```

You will get the following output.

```
09f53738b0cd3bb96f5b1bac488e5528df9906be2480fe61df40e0e0d
19e3d48 Anaconda3-5.2.0-Linux-x86_64.sh
```

4. The fourth step is to run the Anaconda Script, as shown in the following figure.

```
$ bash Anaconda3-5.2.0-Linux-x86_64.sh
```

The command line will generate the following output. You will be asked to review the license agreement. Keep on pressing *Enter* until you reach the end.

```
Output

Welcome to Anaconda3 5.2.0

In order to continue the installation process, please
review the license agreement.
Please, press Enter to continue
>>>
...
Do you approve the license terms? [yes|No]
```

Type, *Yes*, when you get to the bottom of the License Agreement.

5. The installer will ask you to choose the installation location after you agree to the license agreement. Simply press *Enter* to choose the default location. You can also specify a different location if you want.

```
Output

Anaconda3 will now be installed on this location:
/home/tola/anaconda3

- Press ENTER to confirm the location
- Press CTRL-C to abort the installation
- Or specify a different location below

[/home/tola/anaconda3] >>>
```

The installation will proceed once you press *Enter.* Once again, you have to be patient as the installation process takes some time to complete.

6. You will receive the following result when the installation is complete. If you wish to use the conda command, type *Yes*.

```
Output
...
Installation finished.
Do you wish the installer to prepend Anaconda3 install
location to path in your /home/tola/.bashrc? [yes|no]
[no]>>>
```

   At this point, you will also have the option to download the Visual Studio Code. Type *yes* or *no* to install or decline, respectively.

7. Use the following command to activate your brand new installation of Anaconda3.

```
$ source `/.bashrc
```

8. You can also test the installation using the conda command.

```
$ conda list
```

Congratulations. You have successfully installed Anaconda on your Linux system.

1.3.4. Using Google Colab Cloud Environment

In addition to local Python environments such as Anaconda, you can run deep learning applications on Google Colab, as well, which is Google's platform for deep learning with GPU support. All the codes in this book have been run using Google Colab. Therefore I would suggest that you use Google Colab, too.

To run deep learning applications via Google Colab, all you need is a Google/Gmail account. Once you have a Google/Gmail account, you can simply go to:

https://colab.research.google.com/

Next, click on File -> New notebook, as shown in the following screenshot.

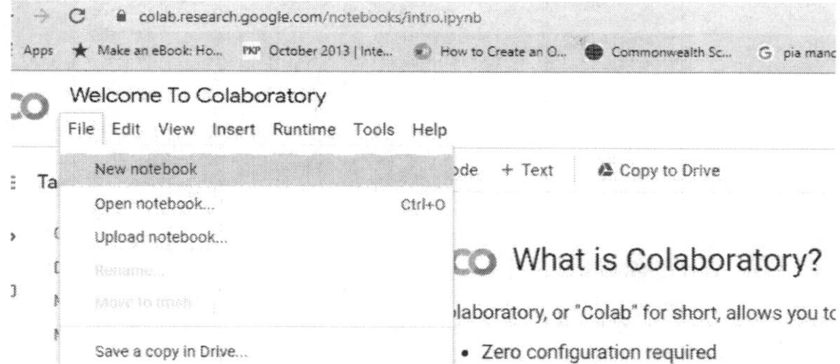

Next, to run your code using GPU, from the top menu, select Runtime -> Change runtime type, as shown in the following screenshot:

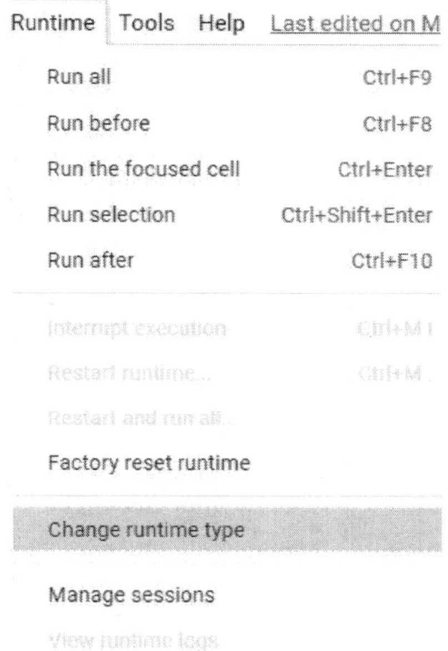

You should see the following window. Here from the dropdown list, select GPU, and click the *Save* button.

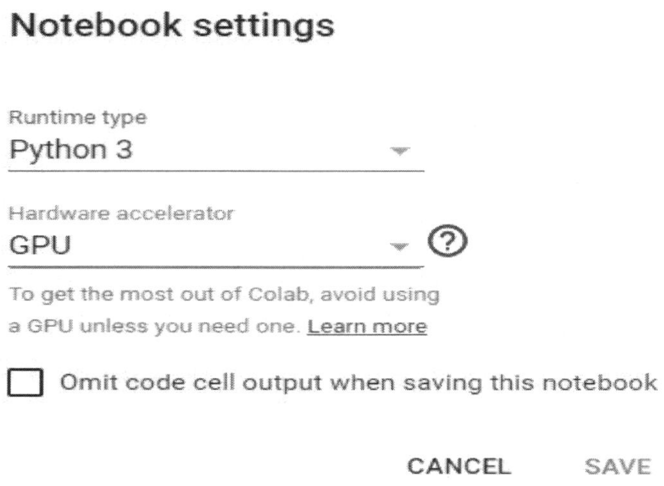

Notebook settings

Runtime type
Python 3

Hardware accelerator
GPU

To get the most out of Colab, avoid using a GPU unless you need one. Learn more

☐ Omit code cell output when saving this notebook

CANCEL SAVE

To make sure you are running the latest version of TensorFlow, execute the following script in the Google Colab notebook cell. The following script will update your TensorFlow version.

```
pip install --upgrade tensorflow
```

To check if you are really running TensorFlow version > 2.0, execute the following script.

```
import tensorflow as tf
print(tf.__version__)
```

With Google Cloud, you can import the datasets from your Google drive. Execute the following script. And click on the link that appears, as shown below:

```
from google.colab import drive
drive.mount('/gdrive')
```

```
Go to this URL in a browser: https://accounts.google.com/o/oauth2/auth

Enter your authorization code:
```

You will be prompted to allow Google Colab to access your Google drive. Click the *Allow* button, as shown below:

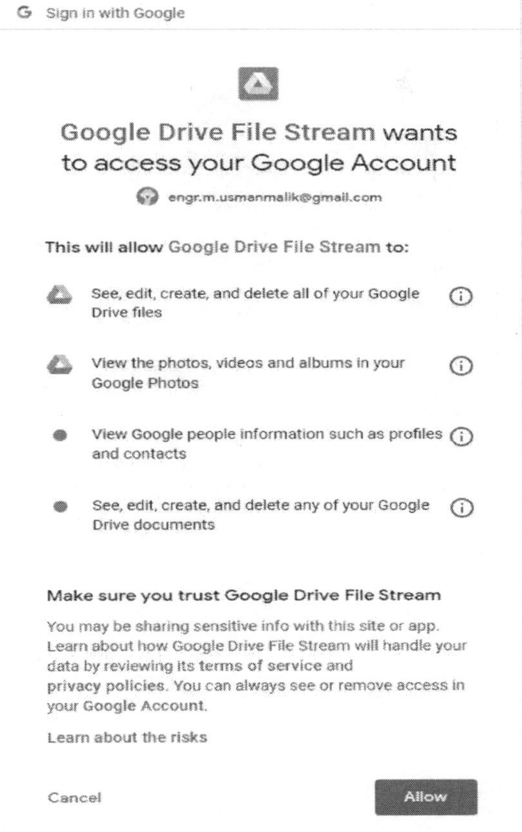

You will see a link appear, as shown in the following image (the link has been blinded here).

Sign in

Please copy this code, switch to your application and paste it there:

Copy the link and paste it in the empty field in the Google Colab cell, as shown below:

```
from google.colab import drive
drive.mount('/gdrive')
```

```
Go to this URL in a browser: https://accounts.google.com/o/oauth2/auth

Enter your authorization code:
```

This way, you can import datasets from your Google drive to your Google Colab environment.

In the next chapter, you will see how to write your first program in Python, along with other Python programming concepts.

CHAPTER

2

Python Crash Course

If you are familiar with the elementary concepts of Python programming language, you can skip this chapter. For those who are absolute beginners to Python, this section provides a very brief overview of some of the most basic concepts of Python. Python is a very vast programming language, and this section is by no means a substitute for a complete Python Book. However, if you want to see how various operations and commands are executed in Python, you are welcome to follow along the rest of this section.

2.1. Writing Your First Program

You have now installed Python on your computer and established a unique environment in the form of Anaconda. It is time to write your first program, that is, Hello World!

In order to write a program in Anaconda, you have to launch Anaconda Navigator. Search *Anaconda Navigator* in your Windows Search Box. Now, click on the Anaconda Navigator application icon, as shown in the following figure.

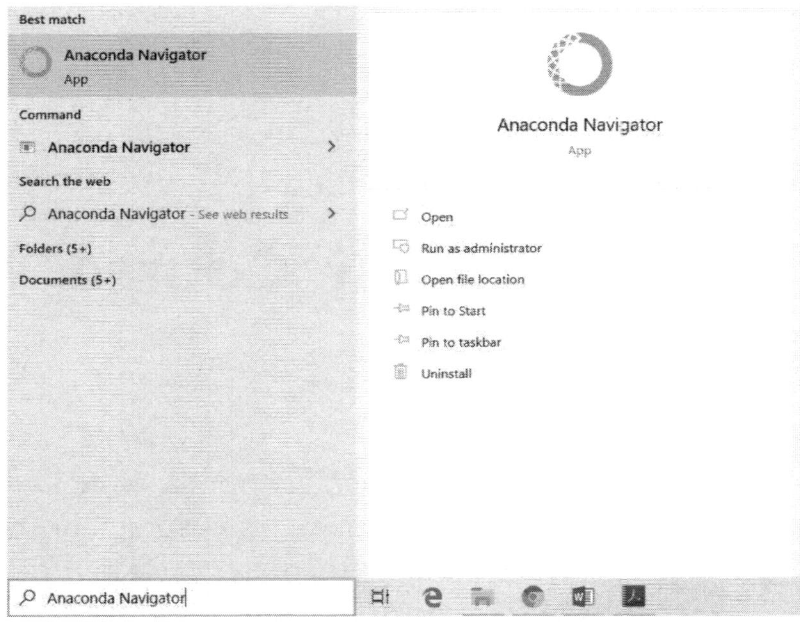

Once you click on the application, Anaconda's dashboard will open. The dashboard offers you a myriad of tools to write your code. We will use the *Jupyter Notebook*, the most popular of these tools, to write and explain the code throughout this book.

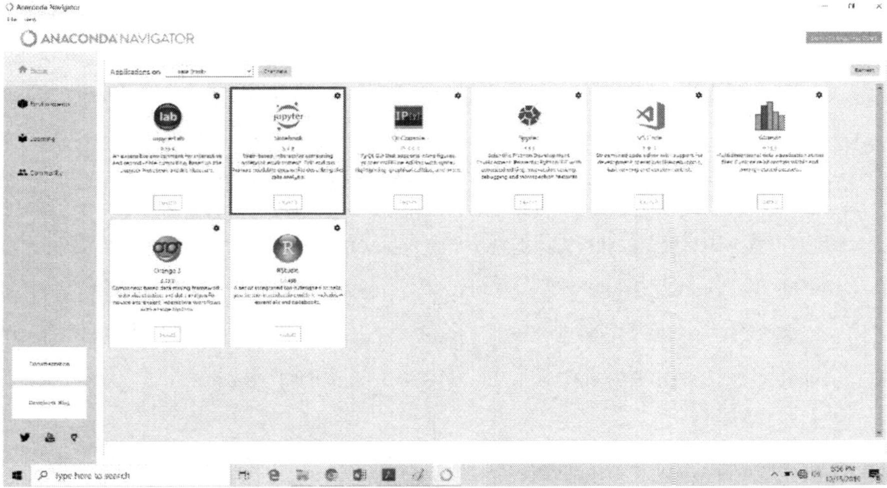

The Jupyter Notebook is available at second from the top of the dashboard. You can use Jupyter Notebook even if you don't have access to the internet as it runs right in your default browser. Another method to open Jupyter Notebook is to type Jupyter Notebook in the Windows search bar. Subsequently, click on the *Jupyter Notebook* application. The application will open in a new tab of your browser.

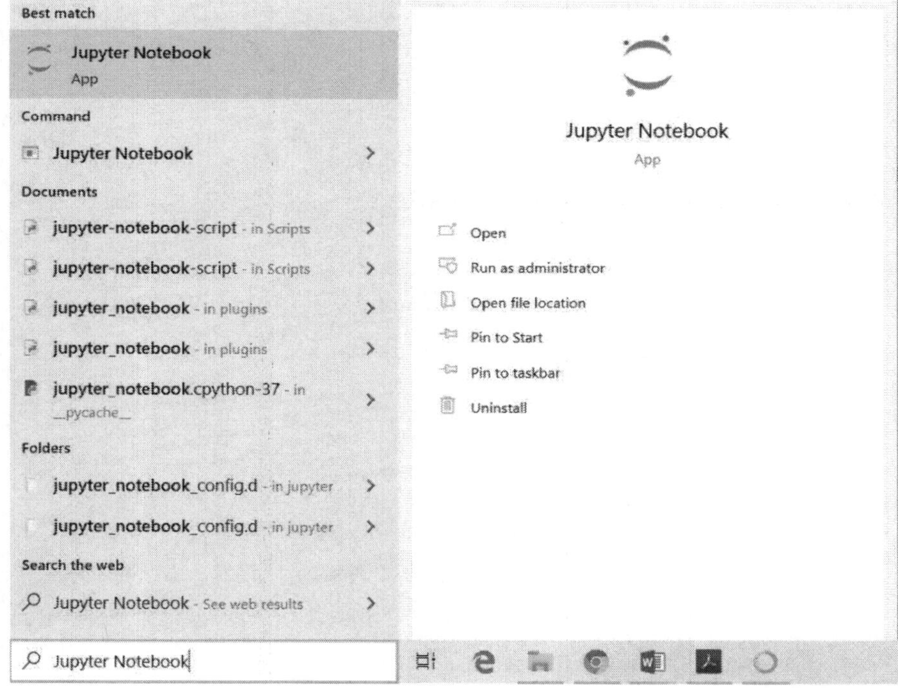

The top right corner of Jupyter Notebook's own dashboard houses a *New* button, which you have to click to open a new document. A dropdown containing several options will appear. Click on Python 3.

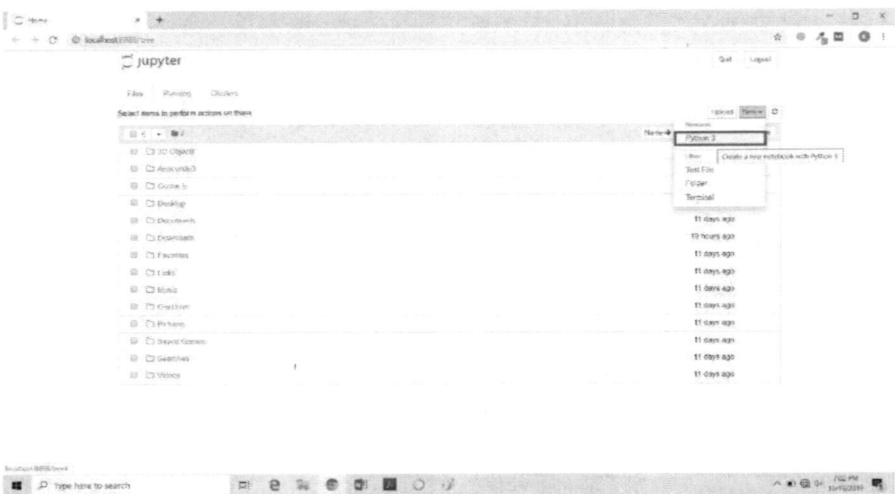

A new Python notebook will appear for you to write your programs. It looks as follows.

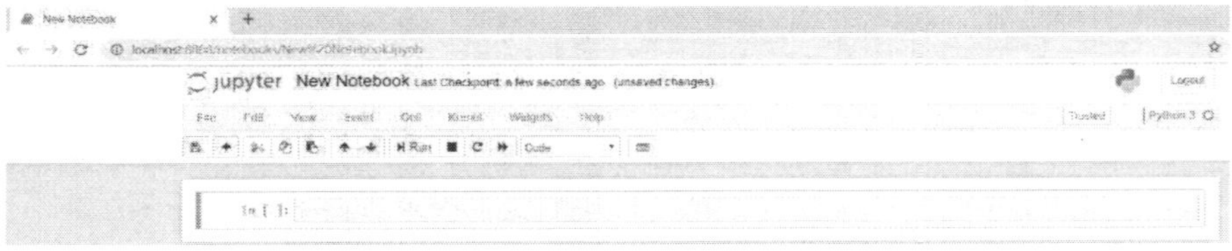

Jupyter Notebook consists of cells, as evident from the above image, making its layout very simple and straightforward. You will write your code inside these cells. Let us write our first ever Python program in Jupyter Notebook.

1.3.1. Writing Your First Program

```
In [1]: print("Welcome to Data Visualization with Python")

        Welcome to Data Visualization with Python
```

The above script basically prints a string value in the output using the **print()** method. The **print()** method is used to print on the console, any string passed to it. If you see the following output, you have successfully run your first Python program.

Output:

```
Welcome to Data Visualization with Python
```

Let's now explore some of the other important Python concepts starting with Variables and Data Types.

Requirements – Anaconda, Jupyter, and Matplotlib

- Each script in this book has been executed via Jupyter Notebook. So, install Jupyter Notebook on your system.

Hands-on Time – Source Codes

All IPython Notebooks for the source code of all the scripts in this chapter can be found in Source Codes/Chapter 2 folder in GitHub and SharePoint repositories. I would suggest that you write all the code in this chapter yourself and see if you can get the same output as mentioned in this chapter.

2.2. Python Variables and Data Types

Data types in a programming language refer to the type of data that the language is capable of processing. The following are the major data types supported by Python:

a. Strings

b. Integers

c. Floating Point Numbers

d. Booleans

e. Lists

f. Tuples

g. Dictionaries

A variable is an alias for the memory address where actual data is stored. The data or the values stored at a memory address can be accessed and updated via the variable name. Unlike other programming languages like C++, Java, and C#, Python is loosely typed, which means that you don't have to specify the data type while creating a variable. Rather, the type of data is evaluated at runtime.

The following example shows how to create different data types and how to store them in their corresponding variables. The script also prints the type of the variables via the **type()** function.

Script 2:

```
# A string Variable
first_name = "Joseph"
print(type(first_name))

# An Integer Variable
age = 20
print(type(age))

# A floating point variable
weight = 70.35
print(type(weight))

# A boolean variable
married = False
print(type(married))

#List
cars = ["Honda", "Toyota", "Suzuki"]
print(type(cars))

```

```
#Tuples
days = ("Sunday", "Monday", "Tuesday", "Wednesday",
    "Thursday", "Friday", "Saturday")
print(type(days))

#Dictionaries
days2 = {1:"Sunday", 2:"Monday", 3:"Tuesday",
    4:"Wednesday", 5:"Thursday", 6:"Friday", 7:"Saturday"}
print(type(days2))
```

Output:

```
<class 'str'>
<class 'int'>
<class 'float'>
<class 'bool'>
<class 'list'>
<class 'tuple'>
<class 'dict'>
```

2.3. Python Operators

Python programming language contains the following types of operators:

a. Arithmetic Operators

b. Logical Operators

c. Comparison Operators

d. Assignment Operators

e. Membership Operators

Let's briefly review each of these types of operators.

Arithmetic Operators

Arithmetic operators are used to perform arithmetic operations in Python. The following table sums up the arithmetic operators supported by Python. Suppose X = 20, and Y = 10.

Operator Name	Symbol	Functionality	Example
Addition	+	Adds the operands on either side	X+ Y= 30
Subtraction	–	Subtracts the operands on the right from the operand on the left side of the subtraction operator	X –Y= 10
Multiplication	*	Multiplies the operands on either side	X * Y= 200
Division	/	Divides the operand on the left by the one on the right	X / Y= 2.0
Modulus	%	Divides the operand on the left by the one on the right and returns the remainder	X % Y= 0
Exponent	**	Takes exponent of the operand on the left to the power of right	X ** Y = 1024 x e^{10}

Here is an example of arithmetic operators with output:

Script 3:

```
X = 20
Y = 10
print(X + Y)
print(X - Y)
print(X * Y)
print(X / Y)
print(X ** Y)
```

Output:

```
30
10
200
2.0
10240000000000
```

Logical Operators

Logical operators are used to perform logical **AND, OR**, and **NOT** operations in Python. The following table summarizes the logical operators. Here, **X** is **True,** and **Y** is **False**.

Operator	Symbol	Functionality	Example
Logical AND	and	If both the operands are true, then the condition becomes true.	(X and Y) = False
Logical OR	or	If any of the two operands are true, then the condition becomes true.	(X or Y) = True
Logical NOT	not	Used to reverse the logical state of its operand.	not(X and Y) =True

Here is an example that explains the usage of the Python logical operators.

Script 4:

```
X = True
Y = False
print(X and Y)
print(X or Y)
print(not(X and Y))
```

Output:

```
False
True
True
```

Comparison Operators

Comparison operators, as the name suggests, are used to compare two or more than two operands. Depending upon the relation between the operands, comparison operators return Boolean values. The following table summarizes comparison operators in Python. Here, X is 20, and Y is 35.

Operator	Symbol	Description	Example
Equality	==	Returns true if values of both the operands are equal	(X == Y) = false
Inequality	!=	Returns true if values of both the operands are not equal	(X = Y) = true
Greater than	>	Returns true if the value of the left operand is greater than the right one	(X> Y) = False
Smaller than	<	Returns true if the value of the left operand is smaller than the right one	(X< Y) = True
Greater than or equal to	>=	Returns true if the value of the left operand is greater than or equal to the right one	(X > =Y) = False
Smaller than or equal to	<=	Returns true if the value of the left operand is smaller than or equal to the right one	(X<= Y) = True

The comparison operators have been demonstrated in action in the following example:

Script 5

```
X = 20
Y = 35

print(X == Y)
print(X != Y)
print(X > Y)
print(X < Y)
print(X >= Y)
print(X <= Y)
```

Output:

```
False
True
False
True
False
True
```

Assignment Operators

Assignment operators are commonly used to assign values to variables. The following table summarizes the assignment operators. Here, X is 20, and Y is equal to 10.

Operator	Symbol	Description	Example
Assignment	=	Used to assign the value of the right operand to the right.	R = X+ Y assigns 30 to R
Add and assign	+=	Adds the operands on either side and assigns the result to the left operand	X += Y assigns 30 to X
Subtract and assign	-=	Subtracts the operands on either side and assigns the result to the left operand	X -= Y assigns 10 to X

Multiply and Assign	*=	Multiplies the operands on either side and assigns the result to the left operand	X *= Y assigns 200 to X
Divide and Assign	/=	Divides the operands on the left by the right and assigns the result to the left operand	X/= Y assigns 2 to X
Take modulus and assign	%=	Divides the operands on the left by the right and assigns the remainder to the left operand	X %= Y assigns 0 to X
Take exponent and assign	**=	Takes exponent of the operand on the left to the power of right and assigns the remainder to the left operand	X **= Y assigns 1024 x e^{10} to X

Take a look at script 6 to see Python assignment operators in action.

Script 6:

```
X = 20; Y = 10
R = X + Y
print(R)

X = 20;
Y = 10
X += Y
print(X)

X = 20;
Y = 10
X -= Y
print(X)

X = 20;
Y = 10
```

```
X *= Y
print(X)

X = 20;
Y = 10
X /= Y
print(X)

X = 20;
Y = 10
X %= Y
print(X)

X = 20;
Y = 10
X **= Y
print(X)
```

Output:

```
30
30
10
200
2.0
0
10240000000000
```

Membership Operators

Membership operators are used to find if an item is a member of a collection of items or not. There are two types of membership operators: the **in** operator and the **not in** operator. The following script shows the **in** operator in action.

Script 7:

```
days = ("Sunday", "Monday", "Tuesday", "Wednesday",
"Thursday", "Friday", "Saturday")
print('Sunday' in days)
```

Output:

```
True
```

And here is an example of the **not in** operator.

Script 8:

```
days = ("Sunday", "Monday", "Tuesday", "Wednesday", "Thursday", "Friday", "Saturday")
print('Xunday' not in days)
```

Output:

```
True
```

2.4. Conditional Statements

Conditional statements in Python are used to implement conditional logic in Python. Conditional statements help you decide whether to execute a certain code block or not. There are three main types of conditional statements in Python:

a. If statement

b. If-else statement

c. If-elif statement

IF Statement

If you have to check for a single condition and you do not concern about the alternate condition, you can use the **if** statement. For instance, if you want to check if 10 is greater than 5 and based on that you want to print a statement, you can use the if statement. The condition evaluated by the **if** statement returns a Boolean value. If the condition evaluated by the **if** statement is true, the code block that follows the **if** statement executes. It is important to mention that in Python, a new code block starts at a new line with on tab indented from the left when compared with the outer block.

Here, in the following example, the condition 10 > 5 is evaluated, which returns true. Hence, the code block that follows the **if** statement executes, and a message is printed on the console.

Script 9:

```
# The if statement

if 10 > 5:
    print("Ten is greater than 10")
```

Output:

```
Ten is greater than 10
```

IF-Else Statement

The **If-else** statement comes in handy when you want to execute an alternate piece of code in case the condition for the if statement returns false. For instance, in the following example, the condition 5 < 10 will return false. Hence, the code block that follows the **else** statement will execute.

Script 10:

```
# if-else statement

if  5 > 10:
    print("5 is greater than 10")
else:
    print("10 is greater than 5")
```

Output:

```
10 is greater than 5
```

IF-Elif Statement

The **`if-elif`** statement comes in handy when you have to evaluate multiple conditions. For instance, in the following example, we first check if 5 > 10, which evaluates to false. Next, an **`elif`** statement evaluates the condition 8 < 4, which also returns false. Hence, the code block that follows the last **`else`** statement executes.

Script 11:

```
#if-elif and else

if  5 > 10:
    print("5 is greater than 10")
elif 8 < 4:
    print("8 is smaller than 4")
else:
    print("5 is not greater than 10 and 8 is not smaller than 4")
```

Output:

```
5  is not greater than 10, and 8 is not smaller than 4
```

2.5. Iteration Statements

Iteration statements, also known as loops, are used to iteratively execute a certain piece of code. There are two main types of iteration statements in Python.

a. For loop

b. While Loop

For Loop

The **`for loop`** is used to iteratively execute a piece of code for a certain number of times. You should use **`for loop`** when you exactly know the number of iterations or repetitions for which you want to run your code. A **for loop** iterates over a collection of items. In the following example, we create a collection of five integers using the **range()** method. Next, a **for loop** iterates five times and prints each integer in the collection.

Script 12:

```
items = range(5)
for item in items:
    print(item)
```

Output:

```
0
1
2
3
4
```

While Loop

The **while loop** keeps executing a certain piece of code unless the evaluation condition becomes false. For instance, the **while loop** in the following script keeps executing unless variable c becomes greater than 10.

Script 13:

```
c = 0
while c < 10:
    print(c)
    c = c +1
```

Output:

```
0
1
2
3
4
5
6
7
8
9
```

2.6. Functions

Functions in any programming language are typically used to implement the piece of code that is required to be executed multiple times at different locations in the code. In such cases, instead of writing long pieces of code again and again, you can simply define a function that contains the piece of code, and then, you can call the function wherever you want in the code.

The def keyword is used to create a function in Python, followed by the name of the function and opening and closing parenthesis.

Once a function is defined, you have to call it in order to execute the code inside a function body. To call a function, you simply have to specify the name of the function, followed by opening and closing parenthesis. In the following script, we create a function named **myfunc**, which prints a simple statement on the console using the **print()** method.

Script 14:

```
def myfunc():
    print("This is a simple function")

### function call
myfunc()
```

Output:

```
This is a simple function
```

You can also pass values to a function. The values are passed inside the parenthesis of the function call. However, you must specify the parameter name in the function definition, too. In the following script, we define a function named **myfuncparam()**. The function accepts one parameter, i.e., **num**. The value passed in the parenthesis of the function call will be stored in this **num** variable and will be printed by the **print()**method inside the **myfuncparam()** method.

Script 15:

```
def myfuncparam(num):
    print("This is a function with parameter value: "+num)

### function call
myfuncparam("Parameter 1")
```

Output:

```
This is a function with parameter value:Parameter 1
```

Finally, a function can also return values to the function call. To do so, you simply have to use the return keyword, followed by the value that you want to return. In the following script, the **myreturnfunc()** function returns a string value to the calling function.

Script 16:

```
def myreturnfunc():
    return "This function returns a value"

val = myreturnfunc()
print(val)
```

Output:

```
This function returns a value
```

2.7. Objects and Classes

Python supports object-oriented programming (OOP). In OOP, any entity that can perform some function and have some attributes is implemented in the form of an object.

For instance, a car can be implemented as an object since a car has some attributes such as price, color, model, and can perform some functions such as drive car, change gear, stop car, etc.

Similarly, a fruit can also be implemented as an object since a fruit has a price, name, and you can eat a fruit, grow a fruit, and perform functions with a fruit.

To create an object, you first have to define a class. For instance, in the following example, a class **Fruit** has been defined. The class has two attributes, **name** and **price**, and one method, **eat_fruit()**. Next, we create an object **f** of class Fruit, and then, we call the **eat_fruit()** method from the **f** object. We also access the **name** and **price** attributes of the **f** object and print them on the console.

Script 17:

```
class Fruit:

    name = "apple"
    price = 10

    def eat_fruit(self):
        print("Fruit has been eaten")


f = Fruit()
f.eat_fruit()
print(f.name)
print(f.price)
```

Output:

```
Fruit has been eaten
apple
10
```

A class in Python can have a special method called the *constructor*. The name of the constructor method in Python is **`__init__()`**. The constructor is called whenever an object of a class is created. Look at the following example to see the constructor in action.

Script 18:

```
class Fruit:

    name = "apple"
    price = 10

    def __init__(self, fruit_name, fruit_price):
        Fruit.name = fruit_name
        Fruit.price = fruit_price

```

```
    def eat_fruit(self):
        print("Fruit has been eaten")


f = Fruit("Orange", 15)
f.eat_fruit()
print(f.name)
print(f.price)
```

Output:

```
Fruit has been eaten
Orange
15
```

Further Readings - Python [1]

To study more about Python, please check Python 3 Official Documentation. Get used to searching and reading this documentation. It is a great resource of knowledge.

2.8. Data Science and Machine Learning Libraries

Owing to the growing importance of data science and machine learning techniques, several Python libraries have been developed. Some of these libraries have been briefly reviewed in this section.

2.8.1. NumPy

NumPy is one of the most commonly used libraries for numeric and scientific computing. NumPy is extremely fast and contains support for multiple mathematical domains, such as linear algebra, geometry, etc. It is extremely important to learn NumPy in case if you plan to make a career in data science and data preparation.

To know more about NumPy, check this link:

https://numpy.org/

2.8.2. Matplotlib

Matplotlib is the de facto standard for static data visualization in Python, which is the first step in data science and machine learning. Being the oldest data visualization library in Python, Matplotlib is the most widely used data visualization library.

Matplotlib was developed to resemble MATLAB, which is one of the most widely used programming languages in academia. While Matplotlib graphs are easy to plot, the look and feel of the Matplotlib plots have a distinct feel of the 1990s. Many wrapper libraries like Pandas and Seaborn have been developed on top of Matplotlib. These libraries allow users to plot much cleaner and sophisticated graphs.

To study more about Matplotlib, check this link:

https://matplotlib.org/

2.8.3. Seaborn

Seaborn library is built on top of the Matplotlib library and contains all the plotting capabilities of Matplotlib. However, with Seaborn, you can plot much more pleasing and aesthetic graphs with the help of Seaborn default styles and color palettes.

To study more about Seaborn, check this link:

https://seaborn.pydata.org/

2.8.4. Pandas

Pandas library, like Seaborn, is based on the Matplotlib library and offers utilities that can be used to plot different types of static plots in a single line of codes. With Pandas, you can import data in various formats such as CSV (Comma Separated View) and TSV (Tab Separated View) and can plot a variety of data visualizations via these data sources.

To know more about Seaborn, check this link:

https://pandas.pydata.org/

2.8.5. Scikit Learn

Scikit Learn, also called sklearn, is an extremely useful library for data science and machine learning in Python. Sklearn contains many built-in modules that can be used to perform data preparation tasks, such as feature engineering, feature scaling, outlier detection, discretization, etc. You will be using Sklearn a lot in this book. Therefore, it can be a good idea to study sklearn before you start coding using this book.

To study more about Scikit Learn, check this link:

https://scikit-learn.org/stable/

2.8.6. TensorFlow

TensorFlow is one of the frequently used libraries for deep learning. TensorFlow has been developed by Google and offers an easy to use API for the development of various deep learning models. TensorFlow is consistently being updated, and at the time of writing of this book, TensorFlow 2 is the latest major release of TensorFlow. With TensorFlow, you can not only easily develop deep learning applications, but you can also deploy them with ease, owing to the deployment functionalities of TensorFlow.

To study more about TensorFlow, check this link:

https://www.tensorflow.org/

2.8.7. Keras

Keras is a high-level TensorFlow library that implements complex TensorFlow functionalities under the hood. If you are a beginner, Keras is the one deep learning library that you should start with to develop a deep learning library. As a matter of fact, Keras has been adopted as the official deep learning library for TensorFlow 2.0, and now, all the TensorFlow applications use Keras abstractions for training deep learning models.

To study more about Keras, check this link:

https://keras.io/

Hands-On Time – Exercise

Now, it is your turn. Follow the instructions in **the exercises below** to check your understanding of basic Python conepts. The answers are given at the end of the book.

You are now familiar with basic Python concepts. In the next section, you will start working on your first machine learning project, where you will predict house prices using linear regression in Scikit learn.

Exercise: Chapter 2.1

Question 1

Which iteration should be used when you want to repeatedly execute a code a specific number of times?

A. For Loop

B. While Loop

C. Both A & B

D. None of the above

Question 2

What is the maximum number of values that a function can return in Python?

A. Single Value

B. Double Value

C. More than two values

D. None

Question 3

Which of the following membership operators are supported by Python?

A. In

B. Out

C. Not In

D. Both A and C

PROJECT

1

House Price Prediction Using Linear Regression

Predicting house prices is one of the most common applications of machine learning algorithms such as linear regression.

Machine learning algorithms can be, on the whole, categorized into two types: Supervised learning and unsupervised learning algorithms.

Supervised machine learning algorithms are those algorithms where the input dataset and the corresponding output or true prediction is available, and the algorithms try to find the relationship between inputs and outputs.

Linear regression, a supervised machine learning algorithm, is trained via correct output labels. Linear regression is a linear model that assumes a linear relationship between inputs and outputs and minimizes the cost of error between the predicted and actual output using functions gradient descent.

Why Use Linear Regression Algorithm?

Linear regression algorithm is particularly useful when:

1. Linear regression is a simple to implement and easily interpretable algorithm.

2. Takes less training time to train even for huge datasets.
3. Linear regression coefficients are easy to interpret.

Disadvantages of Linear Regression Algorithm

The following are the disadvantages of the linear regression algorithm:

1. Performance is easily affected by outlier presence.
2. Assumes a linear relationship between dependent and independent variables, which can result in an increased error.

In this section, you will see how to predict the median value of house prices in different towns of Boston, which is a state in America, using a linear regression algorithm implemented in Python's Scikit-Learn library. So, let's begin without much ado.

Installing the Required Libraries

Before you can go on and train a linear regression algorithm for house price prediction, you need to install a few libraries. On your command terminal, execute the following commands to install the required libraries. You will see the functionalities of these libraries later in this project.

```
pip install scikit-learn
pip install numpy
pip install pandas
pip install matplotlib
pip install seaborn
```

1.1. Importing Libraries

Once the libraries are installed, you have to import them into your Python application, as shown in the following script:

Script 1:

```
import numpy as np
import pandas as pd
import matplotlib.pyplot as plt
import seaborn as sns
from sklearn.model_selection import train_test_split
from sklearn.linear_model import LinearRegression
from sklearn import metrics

%matplotlib inline
```

1.2. Importing the Dataset

Machine learning algorithms require data for training. The dataset that we are going to use to train our linear regression algorithm can be downloaded from this Kaggle link: https://bit.ly/3k9jFLR.

The dataset is also available by the name: BostonHousing.csv in the *Datasets* folder in GitHub and SharePoint repositories. Download the dataset to your local file system, and use the `read_csv()` method of the `Pandas` library to read the dataset into a Pandas dataframe, as shown in the following script. The script also prints the first five rows of the dataset using the `head()` method.

Script 2:

```
housing_dataset = pd.read_csv("E:\Machine Learning and Data Science Projects with Python\Datasets\BostonHousing.csv")
housing_dataset.head()
```

Output:

	crim	zn	indus	chas	nox	rm	age	dis	rad	tax	ptratio	b	lstat	medv
0	0.00632	18.0	2.31	0	0.538	6.575	65.2	4.0900	1	296	15.3	396.90	4.98	24.0
1	0.02731	0.0	7.07	0	0.469	6.421	78.9	4.9671	2	242	17.8	396.90	9.14	21.6
2	0.02729	0.0	7.07	0	0.469	7.185	61.1	4.9671	2	242	17.8	392.83	4.03	34.7
3	0.03237	0.0	2.18	0	0.458	6.998	45.8	6.0622	3	222	18.7	394.63	2.94	33.4
4	0.06905	0.0	2.18	0	0.458	7.147	54.2	6.0622	3	222	18.7	396.90	5.33	36.2

The details of these columns are available on the Kaggle link: (https://bit.ly/3k9jFLR) for the dataset. The column details are copied from the Kaggle link and are mentioned as follows for your reference:

Column Name	Description
CRIM	The per capita crime rate by town
ZN	The proportion of residential land zoned for lots over 25,000 sq.ft.
INDUS	The proportion of non-retail business acres per town
CHAS	Charles River dummy variable (= 1 if tract bounds river; 0 otherwise)
NOX	Nitric oxide concentration (parts per 10 million)
RM	The average number of rooms per dwelling
AGE	The proportion of owner-occupied units built prior to 1940
DIS	The weighted distances to five Boston employment centers
RAD	The index of accessibility to radial highways
TAX	The full-value property-tax rate per $10,000
PTRATIO	The pupil-teacher ratio by town
B	The proportion of blacks by town per 1000
LSTAT	The lower status of the population
MEDV	The median value of owner-occupied homes in $1000s (target)

The MEDV column contains the median value of owner-occupied houses in 1000s, and this is the value that we will be predicting based on the values in the other columns using linear regression.

We can also check the number of records in our dataset using the shape attribute.

Script 3:

```
housing_dataset.shape
```

The output shows that we have 506 records and 14 columns in our dataset.

Output:

```
(506, 14)
```

1.3. Data Visualization

Before training your algorithm on a dataset, it is always a good step to first visualize your dataset and see if you can manually find any trends in the dataset.

Let's first plot the correlation between all the columns in our dataset. You can do so using the `corr()` function of a dataframe, as shown below:

Script 4:

```
plt.rcParams["figure.figsize"] = [8,6]
corr = housing_dataset.corr()
corr
```

The output below shows that the MEDV column has the highest positive correlation of 0.695 with the RM column (average number of rooms per dwelling), which makes sense since houses with more rooms tend to have higher prices. On the other hand, the MEDV column has the highest negative correlation with the LSTATE column, which corresponds to the lower status of the population, which again makes sense since towns with a large ratio lower status population should have cheaper houses.

Output:

	crim	zn	indus	chas	nox	rm	age	dis	rad	tax	ptratio	b	lstat	medv
crim	1.000000	-0.200469	0.406583	-0.055892	0.420972	-0.219247	0.352734	-0.379670	0.625505	0.582764	0.289946	-0.385064	0.455621	-0.388305
zn	-0.200469	1.000000	-0.533828	-0.042697	-0.516604	0.311991	-0.569537	0.664408	-0.311948	-0.314563	-0.391679	0.175520	-0.412995	0.360445
indus	0.406583	-0.533828	1.000000	0.062938	0.763651	-0.391676	0.644779	-0.708027	0.595129	0.720760	0.383248	-0.356977	0.603800	-0.483725
chas	-0.055892	-0.042697	0.062938	1.000000	0.091203	0.091251	0.086518	-0.099176	-0.007368	-0.035587	-0.121515	0.048788	-0.053929	0.175260
nox	0.420972	-0.516604	0.763651	0.091203	1.000000	-0.302188	0.731470	-0.769230	0.611441	0.668023	0.188933	-0.380051	0.590879	-0.427321
rm	-0.219247	0.311991	-0.391676	0.091251	-0.302188	1.000000	-0.240265	0.205246	-0.209847	-0.292048	-0.355501	0.128069	-0.613808	0.695360
age	0.352734	-0.569537	0.644779	0.086518	0.731470	-0.240265	1.000000	-0.747881	0.456022	0.506456	0.261515	-0.273534	0.602339	-0.376955
dis	-0.379670	0.664408	-0.708027	-0.099176	-0.769230	0.205246	-0.747881	1.000000	-0.494588	-0.534432	-0.232471	0.291512	-0.496996	0.249929
rad	0.625505	-0.311948	0.595129	-0.007368	0.611441	-0.209847	0.456022	-0.494588	1.000000	0.910228	0.464741	-0.444413	0.488676	-0.381626
tax	0.582764	-0.314563	0.720760	-0.035587	0.668023	-0.292048	0.506456	-0.534432	0.910228	1.000000	0.460853	-0.441808	0.543993	-0.468536
ptratio	0.289946	-0.391679	0.383248	-0.121515	0.188933	-0.355501	0.261515	-0.232471	0.464741	0.460853	1.000000	-0.177383	0.374044	-0.507787
b	-0.385064	0.175520	-0.356977	0.048788	-0.380051	0.128069	-0.273534	0.291512	-0.444413	-0.441808	-0.177383	1.000000	-0.366087	0.333461
lstat	0.455621	-0.412995	0.603800	-0.053929	0.590879	-0.613808	0.602339	-0.496996	0.488676	0.543993	0.374044	-0.366087	1.000000	-0.737663
medv	-0.388305	0.360445	-0.483725	0.175260	-0.427321	0.695360	-0.376955	0.249929	-0.381626	-0.468536	-0.507787	0.333461	-0.737663	1.000000

In addition to plotting a table, you can also plot a heatmap that shows the correlation between two columns in the form of boxes. To plot a heatmap, you need to pass the output of the `corr()` function of the `Pandas` dataframe to the `heatmap()` function of the `Seaborn` library, as shown below:

Script 5:

```
1. sns.heatmap(corr)
```

Output:

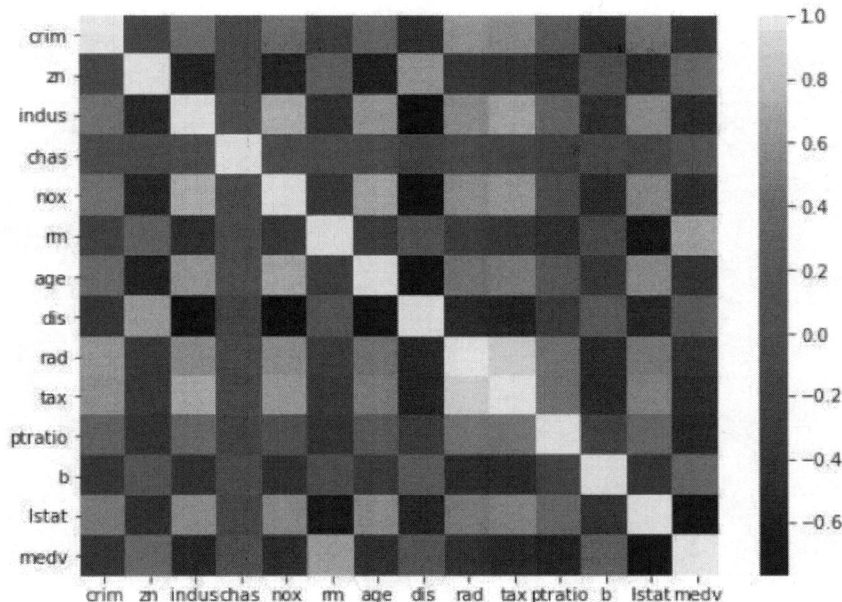

In the above heatmap, the lighter the box, the higher will be the positive correlation, and the darker the box, the higher will be the negative correlation between columns.

1.4. Divide Data into Features and Labels

The next step is to divide data into features and labels set. In our dataset, features consist of all the columns except the MEDV column, while labels consist of the MEDV column. The following script stores features in variable X and labels in variable y. These are the most commonly used names for features and labels. You can use your own names if you like.

Script 6:

```
X = housing_dataset.drop(["medv"], axis  =  1)
y = housing_dataset.filter(["medv"], axis  =  1)
```

Now, if you plot the X dataframe, you will see the feature set, as shown below:

Script 7:

```
X.head()
```

Output:

	crim	zn	indus	chas	nox	rm	age	dis	rad	tax	ptratio	b	lstat
0	0.00632	18.0	2.31	0	0.538	6.575	65.2	4.0900	1	296	15.3	396.90	4.98
1	0.02731	0.0	7.07	0	0.469	6.421	78.9	4.9671	2	242	17.8	396.90	9.14
2	0.02729	0.0	7.07	0	0.469	7.185	61.1	4.9671	2	242	17.8	392.83	4.03
3	0.03237	0.0	2.18	0	0.458	6.998	45.8	6.0622	3	222	18.7	394.63	2.94
4	0.06905	0.0	2.18	0	0.458	7.147	54.2	6.0622	3	222	18.7	396.90	5.33

Similarly, the following script prints the label set.

Script 8:

```
y.head()
```

Output:

	medv
0	24.0
1	21.6
2	34.7
3	33.4
4	36.2

1.5. Divide Data into Training and Test Sets

As I said earlier, after a machine learning algorithm has been trained, it needs to be evaluated to see how well it performs on unseen data. Therefore, we divide the dataset into two sets, i.e., train set and test set.

The dataset is trained via the train set and evaluated on the test set. To split the data into training and test sets, you can use the `train_test_split()` function from the Sklearn library, as shown below. The following script divides the data into 80 percent train set and 20 percent test set since the value for the `test_size` variable is set to 0.2.

Script 9:

```
X_train, X_test, y_train, y_test = train_test_split(X, y,
test_size=0.2, random_state=42)
```

1.6. Training Linear Regression Algorithm

You can code your own Linear Regression algorithm in Python. In addition, you can use any off-the-shelf machine learning library such as Sklearn (Scikit-Learn) to do so.

To implement linear regression with Sklearn, you can use the `LinearRegression` class from the `sklearn.linear_model` module. To train the algorithm, the training and test sets, i.e., `X_train` and `X_test` in our case, are passed to the `fit()` method of the object of the `LinearRegression` class. The test set is passed to the `predict()` method of the class to make predictions. The process of training and making predictions with the linear regression algorithm is as follows:

Script 10:

```
house_predictor = LinearRegression()
house_predictor.fit(X_train, y_train)
y_pred = house_predictor.predict(X_test)
```

1.7. Evaluating the Performance of a Trained Model

Once you have trained a model and have made predictions on the test set, the next step is to know how well your model has performed for making predictions on the unknown test set. There are numerous metrics to evaluate the performance of a regression algorithm, like linear regression. However, mean absolute error, mean squared error, and root mean squared error are three of the most common metrics.

Mean Absolute Error

Mean absolute error (MAE) is calculated by taking the average of absolute error obtained by subtracting the real values from predicted values. The equation for calculating MAE is given below:

$$\text{MAE} = \frac{\sum_{i=1}^{n} |y_i - \hat{y}_1|}{n}$$

Mean Squared Error

Mean squared error (MSE) is similar to MAE. However, error for each record is squared in the case of MSE in order to punish the data record with a huge difference between the predicted and actual values. The equation to calculate the mean squared error is as follows:

$$\text{MSE} = \frac{1}{n} \sum_{i=1}^{n} (y_i - \hat{y})^2$$

Root Mean Squared Error

Root Mean Squared Error is simply the under root of mean squared error and can be calculated as follows:

$$\text{RMSE} = \sqrt{\frac{1}{n}\sum_{i=1}^{n}(y_i - \hat{y})^2}$$

The methods used to find the value for these metrics are available in `sklearn.metrics` class. The predicted and actual values have to be passed to these methods, as shown in the output.

Script 11:

```
print('Mean Absolute Error:', metrics.mean_absolute_error(y_test, y_pred))
print('Mean Squared Error:', metrics.mean_squared_error(y_test, y_pred))
print('Root Mean Squared Error:', np.sqrt(metrics.mean_squared_error(y_test, y_pred)))
```

Output:

```
Mean Absolute Error: 3.1890919658878842
Mean Squared Error: 24.291119474973815
Root Mean Squared Error: 4.928602182665367
```

The MAE value of 3.18 shows that, on average, there is an error of 3.18 dollars between the actual and predicted values for the MEDV column.

The actual and predicted values for the test set can be plotted side by side using the following script:

Script 12:

```
comparison_df = pd.DataFrame({'Actual': y_test.values.tolist(), 'Predicted': y_pred.tolist()})
comparison_df
```

Output:

	Actual	Predicted
0	[23.6]	[28.996723619824973]
1	[32.4]	[36.025565335672255]
2	[13.6]	[14.816944045388373]
3	[22.8]	[25.031979150399543]
4	[16.1]	[18.769879915248175]
...	...	...
97	[17.9]	[-0.16423699568673555]
98	[9.6]	[13.684866815285751]
99	[17.2]	[16.183596971713317]
100	[22.5]	[22.27621999353341]
101	[21.4]	[24.47902363902068]

You can also print the linear regression coefficient of the learned linear regression algorithm to actually see how the linear regression algorithm is making predictions on the test set. To print the linear regression coefficients, you can use the coef_ attribute of the linear regression coefficients.

Script 13:

```
1. print(house_predictor.coef_)
```

Output:

```
[[-1.13055924e-01  3.01104641e-02  4.03807204e-02
   2.78443820e+00
  -1.72026334e+01  4.43883520e+00 -6.29636221e-03
   -1.44786537e+00
   2.62429736e-01 -1.06467863e-02 -9.15456240e-01
   1.23513347e-02
  -5.08571424e-01]]
```

1.8. Making Predictions on a Single Data Point

In this section, you will see how to make predictions on a single data point. Let's print the shape of the feature vector or record at the first index in the test set.

Script 14:

```
X_test.values[1].shape
```

From the output below, you can see that this single record has one dimension.

Output:

```
(13,)
```

To make predictions on a single record, the feature vector for the record should be in the form of a row vector. You can covert the feature vector for a single record into the row vector using the `reshape(1,-1)` method, as shown below:

Script 15:

```
single_point = X_test.values[1].reshape(1,-1)
single_point.shape
```

The output shows that the shape of the feature has now been updated to a row vector.

Output:

```
(1, 13)
```

To make predictions, you simply have to pass the row feature vector to the `predict()` method of the trained linear regressor, as shown below:

Script 16:

```
1. house_predictor.predict(X_test.values[1].reshape(1,-1))
```

The predicted value is 36.02 thousand.

Output:

```
array([[36.02556534]])
```

Let's now print the actual median value for house price for the feature index 1 of the test set.

Script 17:

```
y_test.values[1]
```

The actual value is 32 thousand, which means that our prediction has an error of an estimated 4 thousand.

Output:

```
array([32.4])
```

You can try other regression algorithms from the Sklearn library located at this link (https://scikit-learn.org/stable/supervised_learning.html) and see if you can get a lesser error.

Further Readings – Linear Regression

To know more about linear regression, check out these links:
https://bit.ly/2ZyCa49
https://bit.ly/2H1oo41
https://bit.ly/3lXH1EB

Exercise 1.1

Question 1:

Which attribute of the Linear Regression class is used to print the linear regression coefficients of a trained algorithm:

A. reg_coef
B. coefficients
C. coef_
D. None of the above

Question 2:

To make the prediction on a single data point, the data features should be in the form of a __:

A. column vector
B. row vector
C. row or column vector
D. scalar value

Question 3:

Which of the following is not a metric used to measure the performance of a regression algorithm?

A. Accuracy
B. Mean Absolute Error
C. Mean Squared Error
D. Root Mean Squared Error

PROJECT

2

Filtering Spam Email Messages Using Naïve Bayes Algorithm

If you have used Gmail, Yahoo, or any other email service, you would have noticed that some emails are automatically marked as spam by email engines. These spam email detectors are based on rule-based and statistical machine learning approaches.

Spam email filtering is a text classification task, where based on the text of the email, we have to classify whether or not an email is a spam email. Supervised machine learning is commonly used for classification, particularly if the true outputs are available in the dataset.

The Naïve Bayes Algorithm is one of the supervised machine learning algorithms that have been proven to be effective for spam email detection. In this project, you will see how to detect spam emails using the Naïve Bayes algorithm implemented via Python's Sklearn library.

Why Use Naïve Bayes Algorithm?

Linear regression algorithm is particularly useful when:

1. Performs brilliantly when there is no relationship between attributes in a feature vector.
2. Requires a very small amount of data for training.
3. Very easy to implement and understand.

Disadvantages of Naïve Bayes Algorithm

The following are the disadvantages of the linear regression algorithm:

1. Unable to capture the relationships between various features in a dataset.
2. If a category exists in the test set but not in the training set, the probability of prediction for that category in the test set will be set to 0.

Let's now build a neural network for price prediction.

To install the libraries required for this project, execute the following pip command on your command terminals.

2.1. Installing the Required Libraries

```
pip install scikit-learn
pip install numpy
pip install pandas
pip install matplotlib
pip install seaborn
pip install nltk
pip install regex
pip install wordcloud
```

2.2. Importing the Libraries

The second step is to import the required libraries. Execute the following script to do so:

Script 1:

```
import numpy as np
import pandas as pd
import re
import nltk
import matplotlib.pyplot as plt
import seaborn as sns
from sklearn.naive_bayes import MultinomialNB
from wordcloud import WordCloud
%matplotlib inline
```

2.3. Importing the Dataset

The dataset that we are going to use to train our naïve Bayes algorithm for spam email detection can be downloaded from this Kaggle link: https://bit.ly/3j9Uh7h.

The dataset is also available by the name: *emails.csv* in the data folder in the book resources. Download the dataset to your local file system and use the `read_csv()` method of the `Pandas` library to read the dataset into a Pandas dataframe, as shown in the following script. The script also prints the first five rows of the dataset using the `head()` method.

Script 2:

```
data_path = "E:\Machine Learning and Data Science Projects with Python\Datasets\emails.csv"
message_dataset = pd.read_csv(data_path, engine='python')
message_dataset.head()
```

Output:

	text	spam
0	Subject: naturally irresistible your corporate...	1
1	Subject: the stock trading gunslinger fanny i...	1
2	Subject: unbelievable new homes made easy im ...	1
3	Subject: 4 color printing special request add...	1
4	Subject: do not have money , get software cds ...	1

The above output shows that our dataset contains two columns: text and spam. The text column contains texts of email, and the spam column contains the label 1 or 0, where 1 corresponds to spam emails and 0 corresponds to non-spam or ham emails.

Next, we can plot the shape of our dataset.

Script 3:

```
1. message_dataset.shape
```

The output shows that our dataset contains 5,728 emails.

Output:

```
(5728, 2)
```

2.4. Data Visualization

Data visualization is always a good step before training a machine learning model. We will also do that.

Let's plot a pie chart that shows the distribution of spam and non-spam emails in our dataset.

Script 4:

```
plt.rcParams["figure.figsize"] = [8,10]
message_dataset.spam.value_counts().plot(kind='pie', autopct='%1.0f%%')
```

Output:

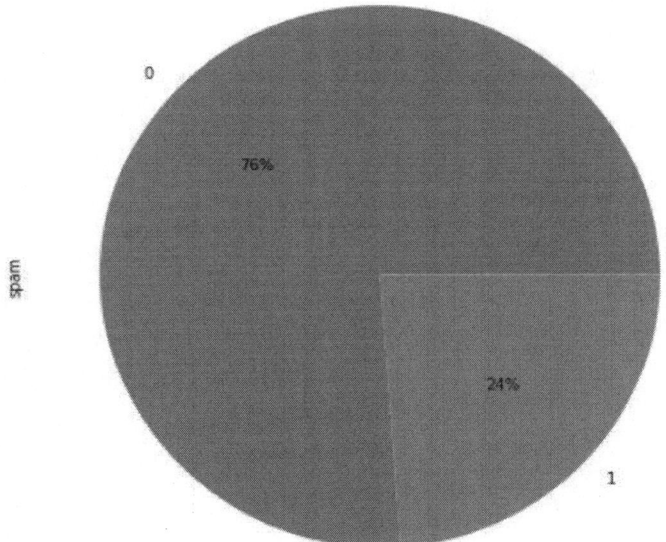

From the above pie chart, you can see that 24 percent of the emails in our dataset are spam emails.

Next, we will plot word clouds for the spam and non-spam emails in our dataset. Word cloud is basically a kind of graph, which shows the most frequently occurring words in the text. The higher the frequency of occurrence, the larger will be the size of the word.

But first, we will remove all the stop words, such as "a, is, you, I, are, etc.," from our dataset because these words occur quite a lot, and they do not have any classification ability. The following script removes all the stop words from the dataset.

Script 5:

```
from nltk.corpus import stopwords
stop = stopwords.words('english')


message_dataset['text_without_sw'] = message_dataset['text'] .apply(lambda x: ' '.join([item for item in x.split() if item not in stop]))
```

The following script filters spam messages from the dataset and then plots word cloud using spam emails only.

Script 6:

```
message_dataset_spam = message_dataset[message_dataset["spam"] == 1]

plt.rcParams["figure.figsize"] = [8,10]
text = ' '.join(message_dataset_spam['text_without_sw'])
wordcloud2 = WordCloud().generate(text)

plt.imshow(wordcloud2)
plt.axis("off")
plt.show()
```

The output below shows that spam emails mostly contain a subject, and they also contain terms like money, free, thank, account, program, service, etc.

Output:

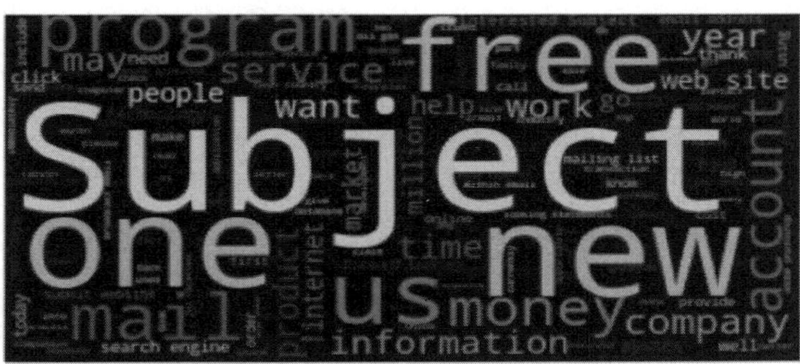

Similarly, the following script plots a word cloud for non-spam emails.

Script 7:

```
message_dataset_ham = message_dataset[message_
dataset["spam"] == 0]

plt.rcParams["figure.figsize"] = [8,10]
text = ' '.join(message_dataset_ham['text_without_sw'])
wordcloud2 = WordCloud().generate(text)

plt.imshow(wordcloud2)
plt.axis("off")
plt.show()
```

You can see that non-spam emails contain mostly informal words such as thank, work, etc., time, need, etc.

Output:

2.5. Cleaning the Data

Before training our machine learning model on the training data, we need to remove the special characters and numbers from our text. Removing special characters and numbers create empty spaces in the text, which also need to be removed.

Before cleaning the data, let's first divide the data into the email text, which forms the feature set (X), and the email labels (y), which contains information about whether or not an email is a spam email.

Script 8:

```
X = message_dataset["text"]
y = message_dataset["spam"]
```

The following script defines a **clean_text()** method, which accepts a text string and returns a string that is cleaned of digits, special characters, and multiple empty spaces.

Script 9:

```
def clean_text(doc):
    document = re.sub('[^a-zA-Z]', ' ', doc)
    document = re.sub(r"\s+[a-zA-Z]\s+", ' ', document)
    document = re.sub(r'\s+', ' ', document)
    return document
```

The following script calls the **clean_text()** method and preprocesses all the emails in the dataset.

Script 10:

```
X_sentences = []
reviews = list(X)
for rev in reviews:
    X_sentences.append(clean_text(rev))
```

2.6. Convert Text to Numbers

Naïve Bayes algorithm is a statistical algorithm. Statistical algorithms work with numbers. Therefore, you need to convert the text of emails into numeric form. There are various ways to do so, e.g., Bag of Words, TFIDF, Word Embeddings, etc. In this section, you will use the TFIDF technique for converting text to numbers.

To use the TFIDF scheme, the **TfIdfVectorizer** class from the **sklearn.feature_extraction.text** is used. You first have to call the **fit()** and then **transform()** method on the text features. Also, you can pass **"stop_words = 'english'"** as an attribute to automatically remove stop words from your text. Look at the following script:

Script 11:

```
from nltk.corpus import stopwords
from sklearn.feature_extraction.text import TfidfVectorizer

vectorizer = TfidfVectorizer (max_features=2500, min_df=5,
max_df=0.7, stop_words=stopwords.words('english'))
X= vectorizer.fit_transform(X_sentences).toarray()
```

In the above script, the **max_features** attribute specifies that a maximum of 2,500 most occurring words should be used to create a feature dictionary. The **min_df** attribute here specifies to only include words that occur for a minimum of five times across all documents. **Max_df** defines not to include words that occur in more than 70 percent of the documents.

2.7. Training the Model

The data is now ready for training a machine learning model. But first, we need to divide our data into the training and test sets. Using the training data, the naïve Bayes algorithm will learn the relationship between the email text and the email label (spam or not) since both email text and corresponding labels are given in the training dataset.

Once the naïve Bayes model is trained on the training set, the test set containing only email texts is passed as inputs to the model. The model then predicts which of the emails in the test set are spam. Predicted outputs for the test set are then compared with the actual label in the test data in order to determine the performance of the spam email detector naïve Bayes model.

The following script divides the data into training and test sets.

Script 12:

```
from sklearn.model_selection import train_test_split
X_train, X_test, y_train, y_test = train_test_split(X, y,
test_size=0.20, random_state=42)
```

To train the machine learning model, you will be using the `MultinomialNB()` class from `sklearn.naive_bayes` module, which is one of the most frequently used machine learning models for classification. The `fit()` method of the `MultinomialNB()` class is used to train the model.

Script 13:

```
spam_detector = MultinomialNB()
spam_detector.fit(X_train, y_train)
```

2.8. Evaluating Model Performance

Once a supervised machine learning model is trained, you can make predictions on the test. To do so, you can use the **`predict()`** method of the `MultinomialNB()`.

Script 14:

```
1. y_pred = spam_detector.predict(X_test)
```

Once you have trained a model and have made predictions on the test set, the next step is to know how well your model has performed for making predictions on the unknown test set. There are various metrics to evaluate a classification method. Some of the most commonly used classification metrics are F1, recall, precision, accuracy, and confusion metric. Before you see the equations for these terms, you need to understand the concept of true positive, true negative, and false positive and false negative outputs:

True Negatives: (TN/tn): True negatives are those output labels that are actually false, and the model also predicted them as false.

True Positive: True positives are those labels that are actually true and also predicted as true by the model.

False Negative: False negatives are labels that are actually true but predicted as false by machine learning models.

False Positive: Labels that are actually false but predicted as true by the model are called false positive.

One way to analyze the results of a classification algorithm is by plotting a confusion matrix, such as the one shown below:

Confusion Matrix

		Predicted Class	
	Total Population n = a number	False (0)	True (1)
Actual Class	False (0)	TN True Negative	FP False Positive
	True (1)	FN False Negative	TP True Positive

Precision

Another way to analyze a classification algorithm is by calculating precision, which is basically obtained by dividing true positives by the sum of true positive and false positive, as shown below:

$$\text{Precision} = \frac{tp}{tp + fp}$$

Recall

Recall is calculated by dividing true positives by the sum of true positive and false negative, as shown below:

$$\text{Recall} = \frac{tp}{tp + fn}$$

F1 Measure

F1 measure is simply the harmonic mean of precision and recall and is calculated as follows:

$$F_1 = \left(\frac{2}{\text{recall}^{-1} + \text{precision}^{-1}}\right) = 2 \cdot \frac{\text{precision} \cdot \text{recall}}{\text{precision} + \text{recall}}$$

Accuracy

Accuracy refers to the number of correctly predicted labels divided by the total number of observations in a dataset.

$$\text{Accuracy} = \frac{tp + tn}{tp + tn + fp + fn}$$

The choice of using a metric for classification problems depends totally upon you. However, as a rule of thumb, in the case of balanced datasets, i.e., where the number of labels for each class is balanced, accuracy can be used as an evaluation metric. For imbalanced datasets, you can use the F1 measure as the classification metric.

The methods used to find the value for these metrics are available in sklearn.metrics class. The predicted and actual values have to be passed to these methods, as shown in the output.

Script 15:

```
from sklearn.metrics import classification_report, confusion_matrix, accuracy_score

print(confusion_matrix(y_test,y_pred))
print(classification_report(y_test,y_pred))
print(accuracy_score(y_test,y_pred))
```

Output:

```
[[849   7]
 [ 18 272]]
              precision    recall  f1-score   support

           0       0.98      0.99      0.99       856
           1       0.97      0.94      0.96       290

    accuracy                           0.98      1146
   macro avg       0.98      0.96      0.97      1146
weighted avg       0.98      0.98      0.98      1146

0.9781849912739965
```

The output shows that our model is 97.81 percent accurate while predicting whether a message is a spam or ham, which is pretty impressive.

2.9. Making Predictions on Single Instance

In addition to making predictions on the complete test set, we can also make predictions on a single sentence. Let's fetch an email randomly from our dataset.

Script 16:

```
print(X_sentences[56])
print(y[56])
```

The text of the email is as follows.

Output:

```
Subject localized software all languages available hello we
would like to offer localized software versions german french
spanish uk and many others all listed software is available
for immediate download no need to wait week for cd delivery
just few examples norton internet security pro windows xp
professional with sp full version corel draw graphics suite
dreamweaver mx homesite includinq macromedia studio mx just
browse our site and find any software you need in your native
language best regards kayleen
1
```

The actual output, i.e., 1, shows that the sentence number 56 in the dataset is 1, i.e., spam. The text of the sentence is also shown in the output.

Let's pass this sentence into our spam detector classifier and see what it thinks:

Script 17:

```
print(spam_detector.predict(vectorizer.transform([X_
sentences[56]])))
```

Output:

```
[1]
```

The model correctly classified the message as spam.

Further Readings – Text Classification

To know more about naïve Bayes text classification problems such as Spam Message filtering, check out these links:
https://bit.ly/3o000jL
https://bit.ly/34b05tb
https://bit.ly/3kbFI9Z

Exercise 2.1

Question 1:

Which attribute of the TfidfVectorizer vectorizer is used to define the minimum word count?

A. min_word

B. min_count

C. min_df

D. None of the above

Question 2:

Which method of the Multinomial NB object is used to train the algorithm on the input data?

A. train()

B. fit()

C. predict()

D. train_data()

Question 3:

Spam email filtering with naive Bayes algorithm is a type of ___ learning problem.

A. Supervised

B. Unsupervised

C. Reinforcement

D. Lazy

PROJECT

Predicting Used Car Sale Price Using Feedforward Artificial Neural Networks

In project 1 of this book, you saw how we can predict the sale prices of houses using linear regression. In this article, you will see how we can use a feedforward artificial neural network to predict the prices of used cars. The car sale price prediction problem is a regression problem like house price prediction since the price of a car is a continuous value.

In this project, you will see how to predict car sale prices using a densely connected neural network (DNN), which is a type of feedforward neural network. Though you can implement a densely connected neural network from scratch in Python, in this project, you will be using the TensorFlow Keras library to implement a feedforward neural network.

What is a FeedForward DNN?

A feedforward densely connected neural network (DNN) is a type of neural network where all the nodes in the previous layer are connected to all the nodes in the subsequent layer of a neural network. A DNN is also called a multilayer perceptron.

A densely connected neural network is mostly used for making predictions on tabular data. Tabular data is the type of data that can be presented in the form of a table.

In a neural network, we have an input layer, one or multiple hidden layers, and an output layer. An example of a neural network is shown below:

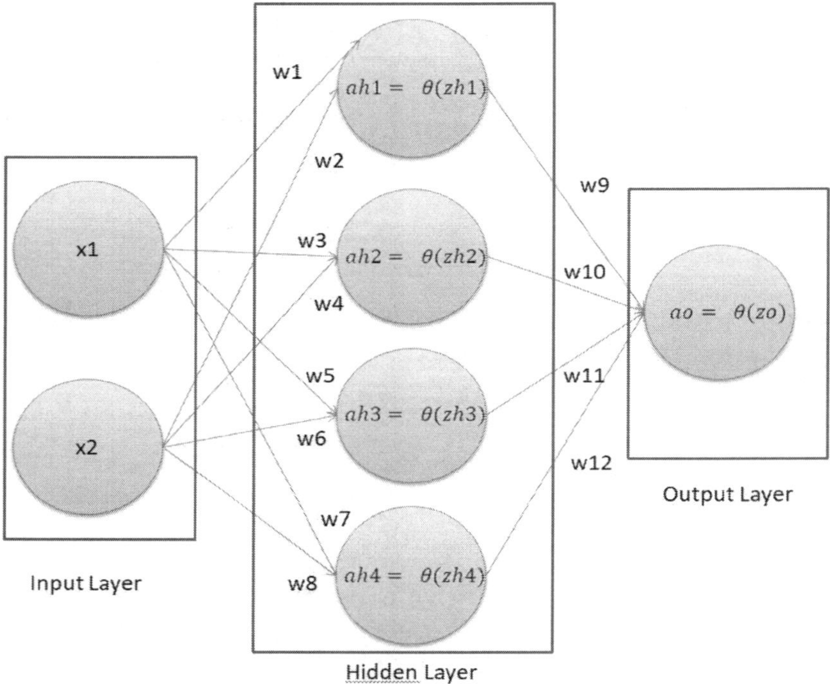

In our neural network, we have two nodes in the input layer (since there are two features in the input), one hidden layer with four nodes, and one output layer with one node since we are doing binary classification. The number of hidden layers and the number of neurons per hidden layer depend upon you.

In the above neural network, x1 and x2 are the input features, and ao is the output of the network. Here, the only thing we can control is the weights w1, w2, w3, ... w12. The idea is to find the values of weights for which the difference between the predicted output, ao, in this case, and the actual output (labels).

A neural network works in two steps:

1. FeedForward
2. BackPropagation

I will explain both these steps in the context of our neural network.

FeedForward

In the feedforward step, the final output of a neural network is created. Let's try to find the final output of our neural network.

In our neural network, we will first find the value of zh1, which can be calculated as follows:

$$zh_1 = x_1 \times w_1 + x_2 \times w_2 + b \quad \text{----------} \ (1)$$

Using zh1, we can find the value of ah1, which is:

$$ah_1 = \frac{1}{\left(1 + e^{-zh_1}\right)} \quad \text{----------} \ (2)$$

In the same way, you find the values of ah2, ah3, and ah4.

To find the value of zo, you can use the following formula:

$$zo = ah_1 \times w_9 + ah_2 \times w_{10} + ah_3 \times w_{11} + ah_4 \times w_{12} \quad \text{----} \ (3)$$

Finally, to find the output of the neural network ao:

$$ao = \frac{1}{\left(1 + e^{-zo}\right)} \quad \text{----------} \ (4)$$

Backpropagation

The purpose of backpropagation is to minimize the overall loss by finding the optimum values of weights. The loss function we are going to use in this section is the mean squared error, which is, in our case, represented as:

$$J = \frac{1}{m}\sum_{i=1}^{m} (ao_i - y_i)^2$$

Here, ao is the predicted output from our neural network, and y is the actual output.

Our weights are divided into two parts. We have weights that connect input features to the hidden layer and the hidden layer to the output node. We call the weights that connect the input to the hidden layer collectively as wh (w1, w2, w3 ... w8), and the weights connecting the hidden layer to the output as wo (w9, w10, w11, and w12).

The backpropagation will consist of two phases. In the first phase, we will find dcost/dwo (which refers to the derivative of the total cost with respect to wo (weights in the output layer)). By the chain rule, dcost/dwo can be represented as the product of dcost/dao * dao/dzo * dzo/dwo (d here refers to derivative). Mathematically:

$$\frac{dcost}{dwo} = \left(\frac{dcost}{dao}\right) \times \left(\frac{dao}{dzo}\right) \times \left(\frac{dzo}{dwo}\right) \text{------ (5)}$$

$$\frac{dcost}{dao} = \frac{1}{m}(ao - y) \text{------- (6)}$$

$$\frac{dao}{dzo} = sigmoid(zo) \times (1 - sigmoid(zo)) \text{--- (7)}$$

$$\frac{dzo}{dwo}=ah.T$$ ----- 8

In the same way, you find the derivative of cost with respect to bias in the output layer, i.e., dcost/dbo, which is given as:

$$\frac{dcost}{dbo}=\left(\frac{dcost}{dao}\right)\times\left(\frac{dao}{dzo}\right)$$

Putting 6, 7, and 8 in equation 5, we can get the derivative of cost with respect to the output weights.

The next step is to find the derivative of cost with respect to hidden layer weights, wh, and bias, bh. Let's first find the derivative of cost with respect to hidden layer weights:

$$\frac{dcost}{dwh}=\left(\frac{dcost}{dah}\right)\times\left(\frac{dah}{dzh}\right)\times\left(\frac{dzh}{dwh}\right)$$ ..... (9)

$$\frac{dcost}{dah}=\left(\frac{dcost}{dao}\right)\times\left(\frac{dao}{dzo}\right)\times\left(\frac{dzo}{dah}\right)$$ .... (10)

The values of dcost/dao and dao/dzo can be calculated from equations 6 and 7, respectively. The value of dzo/dah is given as:

$$\frac{dzo}{dah}=wo.T$$ ...... (11)

Putting the values of equations 6, 7, and 8 in equation 11, you can get the value of equation 10.

Next, let's find the value of dah/dzh:

$$\frac{dah}{dzh}=sigmoid(zh)\times(1\text{-}sigmoid(zh))$$ ..... (12) and,

$$\frac{dzh}{dwh}=X.T$$ ...... (13)

Using equation 10, 12, and 13 in equation 9, you can find the value of dcost/dwh.

Why Use a Linear Feedforward DNN?

A Feedforward DNN has the following advantages:

1. Neural networks produce better results compared to traditional algorithms when you have a large amount of training data.
2. Neural networks are capable of finding hidden features from data that are otherwise not visible to the human eye.

Disadvantages of Feedforward DNN

Following are the disadvantages of neural networks:

1. Require a large amount of training data to produce good results.
2. It can be slow during training time if you have a large number of layers and nodes in your neural network.

In the next steps, you will see how we can create a feedforward densely connected neural network with the TensorFlow Keras library.

3.1. Installing the Required Libraries

If you run the scripts on Google Colab (https://colab.research.google.com/), you do not need to install any library. All the libraries are preinstalled on Google Colab. On the other hand, if you want to run the scripts in this section on your local system or any remote server, you will need to install the following libraries:

```
$pip install scikit-learn
$pip install numpy
$pip install pandas
$pip install matplotlib
$pip install seaborn
```

You also need to install TensorFlow 2.0 to run the scripts. The instructions to download TensorFlow 2.0 are available on their official blog.

3.2. Importing the Libraries

The second step is to import the required libraries. Execute the following script to do so:

Script 1:

```
import pandas as pd
import numpy as np

import matplotlib.pyplot as plt
from sklearn.model_selection import train_test_split
%matplotlib inline

import seaborn as sns
sns.set(style="darkgrid")

import tensorflow as tf
print(tf.__version__)
```

3.3. Importing the Dataset

The dataset that we are going to use to train our feedforward neural network for predicting car sale price can be downloaded from this Kaggle link: https://bit.ly/37E1Ktg. From the above link, download the *train.csv* file only.

The dataset is also available by the name: *car_data.csv* in the Data folder in the book resources. Download the dataset to your local file system, and use the `read_csv()` method of the Pandas library to read the dataset into a Pandas dataframe, as shown in the following script. The following script also prints the first five rows of the dataset using the `head()` method.

Script 2:

```
1. data_path = r"/content/car_data.csv"
2. car_dataset = pd.read_csv(data_path, engine='python')
3. car_dataset.head()
```

Output:

	Unnamed: 0	Name	Location	Year	Kilometers_Driven	Fuel_Type	Transmission	Owner_Type	Mileage	Engine	Power	Seats	New_Price	Price
0	0	Maruti Wagon R LXI CNG	Mumbai	2010	72000	CNG	Manual	First	26.6 km/kg	998 CC	58.16 bhp	5.0	NaN	1.75
1	1	Hyundai Creta 1.6 CRDi SX Option	Pune	2015	41000	Diesel	Manual	First	19.67 kmpl	1582 CC	126.2 bhp	5.0	NaN	12.50
2	2	Honda Jazz V	Chennai	2011	46000	Petrol	Manual	First	18.2 kmpl	1199 CC	88.7 bhp	5.0	8.61 Lakh	4.50
3	3	Maruti Ertiga VDI	Chennai	2012	87000	Diesel	Manual	First	20.77 kmpl	1248 CC	88.76 bhp	7.0	NaN	6.00
4	4	Audi A4 New 2.0 TDI Multitronic	Coimbatore	2013	40670	Diesel	Automatic	Second	15.2 kmpl	1968 CC	140.8 bhp	5.0	NaN	17.74

3.4. Data Visualization and Preprocessing

Let's first see the percentage of the missing data in all the columns. The following script does that.

Script 3:

```
1. car_dataset.isnull().mean()
```

Output:

```
Unnamed: 0           0.000000
Name                 0.000000
Location             0.000000
Year                 0.000000
Kilometers_Driven    0.000000
Fuel_Type            0.000000
Transmission         0.000000
Owner_Type           0.000000
Mileage              0.000332
Engine               0.005981
Power                0.005981
Seats                0.006978
New_Price            0.863100
Price                0.000000
dtype: float64
```

The output above shows that the Mileage, Engine, Power, Seats, and New_Price column contains missing values. The highest percentage of missing values is 86.31 percent, which belongs to the New_Price column. We will remove the New_Price column. Also, the first column, i.e., "Unnamed: 0" doesn't convey any useful information. Therefore, we will delete that column, too. The following script deletes these two columns.

Script 4:

```
1. car_dataset = car_dataset.drop(['Unnamed: 0',  'New_
   Price'], axis = 1)
```

We will be predicting the value in the Price column of the dataset. Let's plot a heatmap that shows a relationship between all the numerical columns in the dataset.

Script 5:

```
1. plt.rcParams["figure.figsize"] = [8 , 6]
2. sns.heatmap(car_dataset.corr())
```

Output:

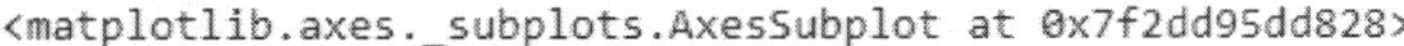

```
<matplotlib.axes._subplots.AxesSubplot at 0x7f2dd95dd828>
```

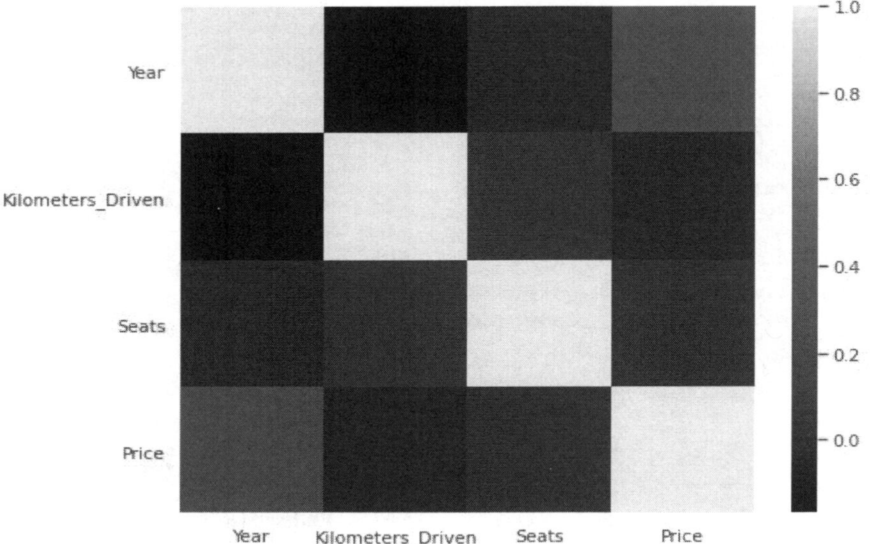

The output shows that there is a very slight positive correlation between the Year and the Price columns, which makes sense as newer cars are normally expensive compared to older cars.

Let's now plot a histogram for the Price to see the price distribution.

Script 6:

```
sns.distplot(car_dataset['Price'])
```

Output:

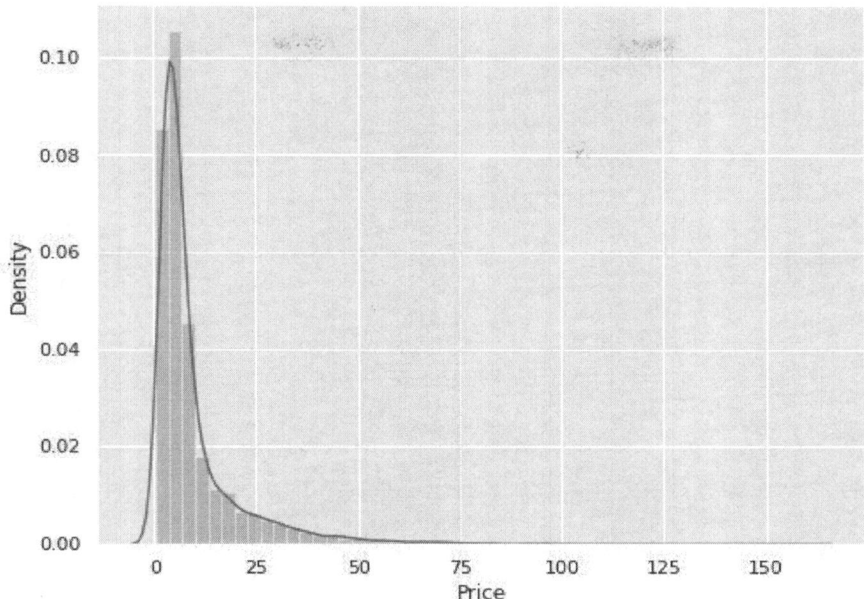

The output shows that most of the cars are priced between 2.5 to 7.5 hundred thousand. Remember, the unit of the price mentioned in the price column is one hundred thousand.

3.5. Converting Categorical Columns to Numerical

Our dataset contains categorical values. Neural networks work with numbers. Therefore, we need to convert the values in the categorical columns to numbers.

Let's first see the number of unique values in different columns of the dataset.

Script 7:

```
car_dataset.nunique()
```

Output:

```
Name                 1876
Location               11
Year                   22
Kilometers_Driven    3093
Fuel_Type               5
Transmission            2
Owner_Type              4
Mileage               442
Engine                146
Power                 372
Seats                   9
Price                1373
dtype: int64
```

Next, we will print the data types of all the columns.

Script 8:

```
print(car_dataset.dtypes)
```

Output:

```
Name                  object
Location              object
Year                   int64
Kilometers_Driven      int64
Fuel_Type             object
Transmission          object
Owner_Type            object
Mileage               object
Engine                object
Power                 object
Seats                float64
Price                float64
dtype: object
```

From the above output, the columns with *object* type are the categorical columns. We need to convert these columns into a numeric type.

Also, the number of unique values in the Name column is too large. Therefore, it might not convey any information for classification. Hence, we will remove the Name column from our dataset.

We will follow a step by step approach. First, we will separate numerical columns from categorical columns. Then, we will convert categorical columns into one-hot categorical columns, and, finally, we will merge the one-hot encoded columns with the original numerical columns. The process of one-hot encoding is explained in a later section.

The following script creates a dataframe of numerical columns only by removing all the categorical columns from the dataset.

Script 9:

```
numerical_data = car_dataset.drop(['Name', 'Location',
'Fuel_Type', 'Transmission', 'Owner_Type',
'Mileage','Engine', 'Power'], axis=1)
numerical_data.head()
```

In the following output, you can see only the numerical columns in our dataset.

Output

	Year	Kilometers_Driven	Seats	Price
0	2010	72000	5.0	1.75
1	2015	41000	5.0	12.50
2	2011	46000	5.0	4.50
3	2012	87000	7.0	6.00
4	2013	40670	5.0	17.74

Next, we will create a dataframe of categorical columns only by filtering all the categorical columns (except Name, since we want to drop it) from the dataset. Look at the following script for reference.

Script 10:

```
1. categorical_data = car_dataset.filter(['Location', 'Fuel_
   Type', 'Transmission', 'Owner_Type', 'Mileage','Engine',
   'Power'], axis=1)
2. categorical_data.head()
```

The output below shows a list of all the categorical columns:

Output:

	Location	Fuel_Type	Transmission	Owner_Type	Mileage	Engine	Power
0	Mumbai	CNG	Manual	First	26.6 km/kg	998 CC	58.16 bhp
1	Pune	Diesel	Manual	First	19.67 kmpl	1582 CC	126.2 bhp
2	Chennai	Petrol	Manual	First	18.2 kmpl	1199 CC	88.7 bhp
3	Chennai	Diesel	Manual	First	20.77 kmpl	1248 CC	88.76 bhp
4	Coimbatore	Diesel	Automatic	Second	15.2 kmpl	1968 CC	140.8 bhp

Now, we need to convert the categorical_data dataframe, which contains categorical values, into numeric form.

One of the most common approaches to convert a categorical column to a numeric one is via one-hot encoding. In one-hot encoding, for every unique value in the original columns, a new column is created. For instance, since the number of unique values in the categorical Transmission column is two, i.e., Manual and Transmission, for the Transmission categorical column in our dataset, two new numeric columns: Transmission_Manual and Transmission_Automatic will be created. If the original Transmission column contained the value Manual, 1 is added in the newly created Transmission_Manual column, while 0 is added in the Transmission_Automatic column.

However, it can be noted that we do not really need two columns. A single column, i.e., Transmission_Manual is enough since when the Transmission is Manual, we can add 1 in the Transmission_Manual column, else 0 can be added in that column. Hence, we actually need N-1 one-hot encoded columns for all the N unique values in the original column.

The following script converts categorical columns into one-hot encoded columns using the `pd.get_dummies()` method.

Script 11:

```
categorical_data__one_hot  = pd.get_dummies(categorical_data, drop_first= True)
categorical_data__one_hot.head()
```

A snapshot of the one-hot encoded columns is shown below.

Output:

Location_Mumbai	Location_Pune	Fuel_Type_Diesel	Fuel_Type_Electric	Fuel_Type_LPG	Fuel_Type_Petrol	Transmission_Manual	Owner_Type_Fourth & Above	Owner_Type_Second	Owner_Type_Third
1	0	0	0	0	0	1	0	0	0
0	1	1	0	0	0	1	0	0	0
0	0	0	0	0	1	1	0	0	0
0	0	1	0	0	0	1	0	0	0
0	0	1	0	0	0	0	0	1	0

Finally, the following script concatenates the numerical columns with one-hot encoded columns to create a final dataset.

Script 12:

```
complete_dataset = pd.concat([numerical_data, categorical_data__one_hot ], axis=1)
complete_dataset.head()
```

Here is the output:

Output:

	Year	Kilometers_Driven	Seats	Price	Location_Bangalore	Location_Chennai	Location_Coimbatore	Location_Delhi	Location_Hyderabad	Location_Jaipur	Location_Kochi
0	2010	72000	5.0	1.75	0	0	0	0	0	0	0
1	2015	41000	5.0	12.50	0	0	0	0	0	0	0
2	2011	46000	5.0	4.50	0	1	0	0	0	0	0
3	2012	87000	7.0	6.00	0	1	0	0	0	0	0
4	2013	40670	5.0	17.74	0	0	1	0	0	0	0

5 rows × 979 columns

Before dividing the data into training and test sets, we will again check if our data contains null values.

Script 13:

```
1. complete_dataset.isnull().mean()
```

Output:

```
Year                    0.000000
Kilometers_Driven       0.000000
Seats                   0.006978
Price                   0.000000
Location_Bangalore      0.000000
                          ...
Power_98.82 bhp         0.000000
Power_98.96 bhp         0.000000
Power_99 bhp            0.000000
Power_99.6 bhp          0.000000
Power_null bhp          0.000000
Length: 979, dtype: float64
```

Now, instead of removing columns, we can remove the rows that contain any null values. To do so, execute the following script:

Script 14:

```
1. complete_dataset.dropna(inplace = True)
```

Before we train our neural network, we need to divide the data into training and test sets, as we did for project 1 and project 2.

3.6. Dividing Data into Training and Test Sets

The following script divides the data into features and labels sets. The Feature set (X in this Project) consists of all the columns except the Price column from the complete_dataset dataframe, while the label set (y in this project) contains the values from the Price column.

Script 15:

```
X = complete_dataset.drop(['Price'], axis=1)
y = complete_dataset['Price']
```

Like traditional machine learning algorithms, neural networks are trained on the training set and are evaluated on the test set. Therefore, we need to divide our dataset into the training and test sets, as shown below:

Script 16:

```
X_train, X_test, y_train, y_test = train_test_split(X, y,
test_size=0.20, random_state=20)
```

To train neural networks, it is always a good approach to scale your feature set. The following script can be used for feature scaling of training and test features.

Script 17:

```
from sklearn.preprocessing import StandardScaler
scaler = StandardScaler()
X_train = scaler.fit_transform(X_train)
X_test = scaler.transform(X_test)
```

3.7. Creating and Training Neural Network Model with Tensor Flow Keras

Now, we are ready to create our neural network in TensorFlow Keras. First, import the following modules and classes.

Script 18:

```
from tensorflow.keras.layers import Input, Dense,
Activation,Dropout
from tensorflow.keras.models import Model
```

The following script describes our neural network. To train a feedforward neural network on tabular data using Keras, you have to first define the input layer using the Input class. The shape of the input in case of tabular data, such as the one we have, should be (Number of Features). The shape is specified by the shape attribute of the Input class.

Next, you can add as many dense layers as you want. In the following script, we add six dense layers with 100, 50, 25, 10, 5, and 2 nodes. Each dense layer uses the relu activation function. The input to the first dense layer is the output from the input layer. The input to each layer is specified in a round bracket that follows the layer name. The output layer in the following script also consists of a dense layer but with 1 node since we are predicting a single value.

Script 19:

```
input_layer = Input(shape=(X.shape[1],))
dense_layer0 = Dense(100, activation='relu')(input_layer)
dense_layer1 = Dense(50, activation='relu')(dense_layer0)
dense_layer2 = Dense(25, activation='relu')(dense_layer1)
dense_layer3 = Dense(10, activation='relu')(dense_layer2)
dense_layer4 = Dense(5, activation='relu')(dense_layer3)
dense_layer5 = Dense(2, activation='relu')(dense_layer4)
output = Dense(1)(dense_layer5)
```

The previous script described the layers. Now is the time to develop the model. To create a neural network model, you can use the Model class from **tensorflow.keras.models** module, as shown in the following script. The input layer is passed to the inputs attribute, while the output layer is passed to the outputs module.

To compile the model, you need to call the compile() method of the model and then specify the loss function, the optimizer, and the metrics. Our loss function is "mean_absolute_error," "optimizer" is adam, and metrics is also the mean absolute error since we are evaluating a regression problem. To study more about Keras optimizers, check this link: https://keras.io/api/optimizers/. And to study more about loss functions, check this link: https://keras.io/api/losses/.

Script 20:

```
model = Model(inputs = input_layer, outputs=output)
model.compile(loss="mean_absolute_error", optimizer="adam", metrics=["mean_absolute_error"])
```

You can also plot and see how your model looks using the following script:

Script 21:

```
from keras.utils import plot_model
plot_model(model, to_file='model_plot.png', show_
shapes=True, show_layer_names=True)
```

You can see all the layers and the number of inputs and outputs from the layers, as shown below:

Output:

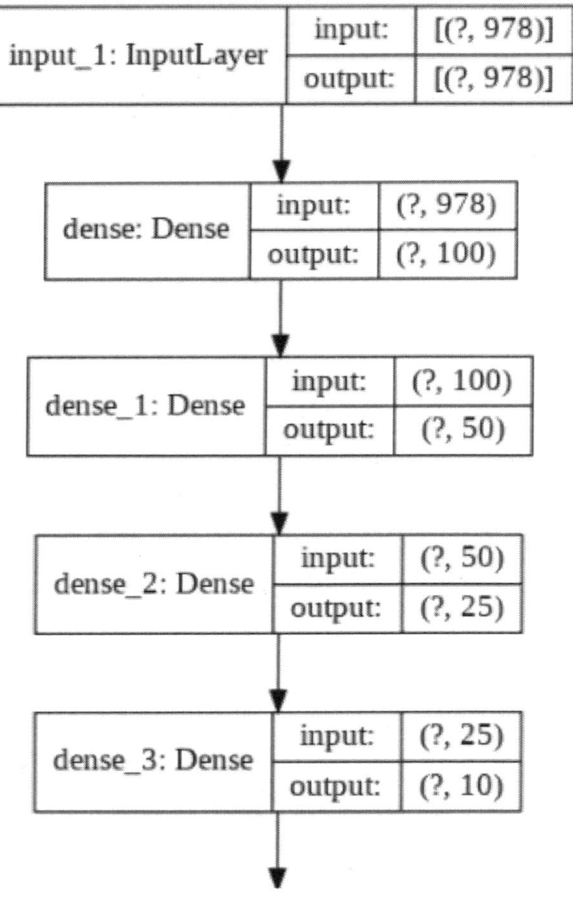

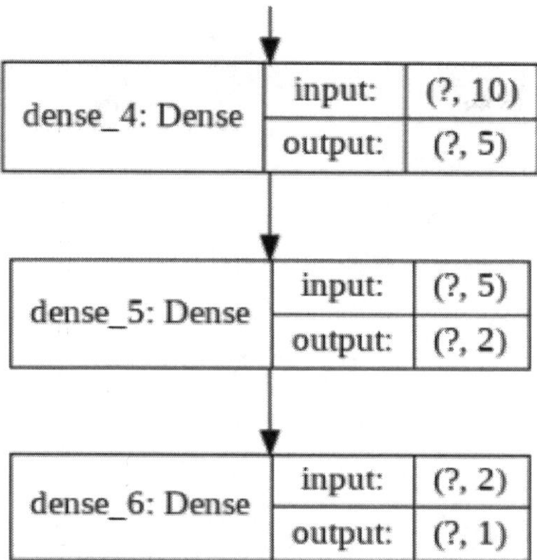

Finally, to train the model, you need to call the fit() method of model class and pass it your training features and test features. Twenty percent of the data from the training set will be used as validation data, while the algorithm will be trained five times on the complete dataset five, as shown by the epochs attribute. The batch size will also be 5.

Script 22:

```
history = model.fit(X_train, y_train, batch_size=5,
epochs=5, verbose=1, validation_split=0.2)
```

The five epochs are displayed below:

Output:

```
Epoch 1/5
765/765 [==============================] - 2s 2ms/step - loss: 3.5883 - mean_absolute_error: 3.5883 - val_loss: 2.5825 - val_mean_absolute_error: 2.5825
Epoch 2/5
765/765 [==============================] - 1s 2ms/step - loss: 2.1662 - mean_absolute_error: 2.1662 - val_loss: 2.2323 - val_mean_absolute_error: 2.2323
Epoch 3/5
765/765 [==============================] - 1s 2ms/step - loss: 1.8443 - mean_absolute_error: 1.8443 - val_loss: 1.8604 - val_mean_absolute_error: 1.8604
Epoch 4/5
765/765 [==============================] - 1s 2ms/step - loss: 1.6240 - mean_absolute_error: 1.6240 - val_loss: 1.9125 - val_mean_absolute_error: 1.9125
Epoch 5/5
765/765 [==============================] - 1s 2ms/step - loss: 1.5245 - mean_absolute_error: 1.5245 - val_loss: 1.7685 - val_mean_absolute_error: 1.7685
```

3.8. Evaluating the Performance of a Neural Network Model

After the model is trained, the next step is to evaluate model performance. There are several ways to do that. One of the ways is to plot the training and test loss, as shown below:

Script 23:

```
plt.plot(history.history['loss'])
plt.plot(history.history['val_loss'])

plt.title('loss')
plt.ylabel('loss')
plt.xlabel('epoch')
plt.legend(['train','test'], loc='upper left')
plt.show()
```

Output:

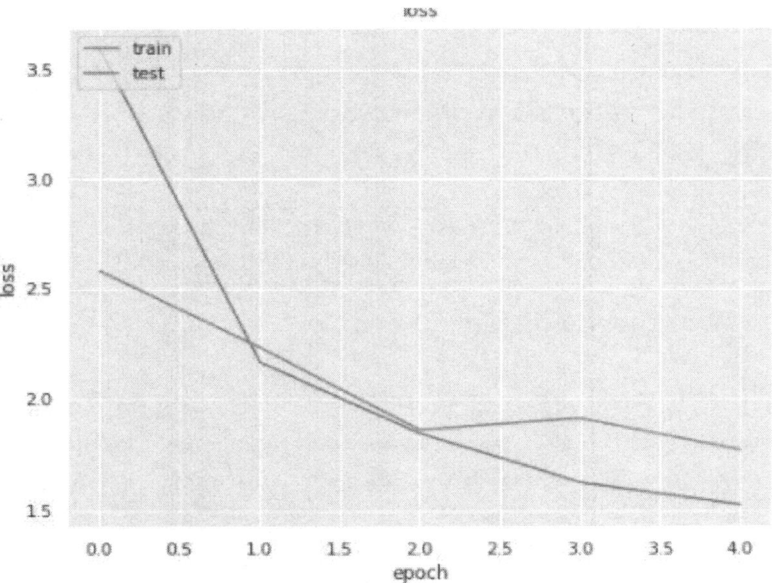

The above output shows that while the training loss keeps decreasing till the fifth epoch, the test or validation loss shows fluctuation after the second epoch, which shows that our model is slightly overfitting.

Another way to evaluate is to make predictions on the test set and then use regression metrics such as MAE, MSE, and RMSE to evaluate model performance.

To make predictions, you can use the predict() method of the model class and pass it the test set, as shown below:

Script 24:

```
y_pred = model.predict(X_test)
```

The following script calculates the values for MAE, MSE, and RMSE on the test set.

Script 25:

```
from sklearn import metrics

print('Mean Absolute Error:', metrics.mean_absolute_
error(y_test, y_pred))
print('Mean Squared Error:', metrics.mean_squared_error(y_
test, y_pred))
print('Root Mean Squared Error:', np.sqrt(metrics.mean_
squared_error(y_test, y_pred)))
```

Output:

```
Mean Absolute Error: 1.869464170857018
Mean Squared Error: 22.80469457178821
Root Mean Squared Error: 4.775426114158632
```

The above output shows that we have a mean error of 1.86. The mean of the Price column can be calculated as follows:

Script 26:

```
car_dataset['Price'].mean()
```

Output:

```
9.479468350224273
```

We can find the mean percentage error by dividing MAE by the average of the Price column, i.e., 1.86/9.47 = 0.196. The value shows that, on average, for all the cars in the test set, the prices predicted by our feedforward neural network and the actual prices differ by 19.6 percent.

You can plot the actual and predicted prices side by side, as follows:

Script 27:

```
1. comparison_df = pd.DataFrame({'Actual': y_test.values.
   tolist(), 'Predicted': y_pred.tolist()})
2. comparison_df
```

Output:

	Actual	Predicted
0	8.25	[9.029337882995605]
1	5.08	[5.067000389099121]
2	4.50	[7.263372898101807]
3	28.50	[22.791542053222656]
4	7.25	[11.030244827270508]
...	...	...
1191	7.50	[6.18602991104126]
1192	21.67	[22.16016387939453]
1193	4.60	[5.486536502838135]
1194	8.00	[15.511911392211914]
1195	2.65	[3.6555228233337402]

1196 rows × 2 columns

3.9. Making Predictions on a Single Data Point

In this section, you will see how to make predictions for a single car price. Let's print the shape of the feature vector or record at the first index in the test set.

Script 28:

```
X_test[1].shape
```

From the output below, you can see that this single record has one dimension.

Output:

```
(978,)
```

As we did in project 1, to make predictions on a single record, the feature vector for the record should be in the form of a row vector. You can covert the feature vector for a single record into the row vector using the `reshape(1,-1)` method, as shown below:

Script 29:

```
single_point = X_test[1].reshape(1,-1)
single_point.shape
```

Output:

```
(1, 978)
```

The output shows that the shape of the feature has now been updated to a row vector.

To make predictions, you simply have to pass the row feature vector to the `predict()` method of the trained neural network model, as shown below:

Script 30:

```
model.predict(X_test[1].reshape(1,-1))
```

The predicted price is 5.06 hundred thousand.

Output:

```
array([[5.0670004]], dtype=float32)
```

The actual price can be printed via the following script:

Script 31:

```
y_test.values[1]
```

Output:

```
5.08
```

The actual output is 5.08 hundred thousand, which is very close to the 5.06 hundred thousand predicted by our model. You can take any other record from the test set, make a prediction on that using the trained neural network, and see how close you get.

Further Readings – TensorFlow Keras Neural

To know more about neural networks in TensorFlow Keras, check out these links:
https://keras.io/
https://www.tensorflow.org/tutorials/keras/regression

Exercise 3.1

Question 1:

In a neural network with three input features, one hidden layer of 5 nodes, and an output layer with three possible values, what will be the dimensions of weight that connects the input to the hidden layer? Remember, the dimensions of the input data are (m,3), where m is the number of records.

A. [5,3]

B. [3,5]

C. [4,5]

D. [5,4]

Question 2:

Which of the following loss functions can you use in case of regression problems?

A. Sigmoid

B. Negative log likelihood

C. Mean Absolute Error

D. Softmax

Question 3:

Neural networks with hidden layers are capable of finding:

A. Linear boundaries

B. Non-linear boundaries

C. All of the above

D. None of the above

PROJECT

Predicting Stock Market Trends with RNN (LSTM)

In project 3, you saw how a feedforward densely connected neural network can be used to make predictions on data that is in the form of tables.

However, in some cases, records in a dataset are sequentially dependent on other records. For instance, consider an example of text. In text, a sentence may depend on the previous sentence. Similarly, stock prices on a particular day are dependent upon the stock prices the day before that day. Feedforward densely connected neural networks are not suitable since they do not have any memory to make predictions for future stock prices or about future sales. We need a neural network that has memory and is capable of remembering what happened at a previous instance.

This is where a Recurrent Neural Network and LSTM come into play. These neural networks are capable of making future predictions based on previous records.

In this project, you will see how to predict one-month future stock prices for Facebook, based on the previous five years of data. But before that, a brief description of Recurrent Neural Networks and LSTM is presented in the next section.

4.1. Recurrent Neural Networks (RNN)

4.1.1. What Is an RNN and LSTM?

This section explains what a recurrent neural network (RNN) is, what is the problem with RNN, and how a long short-term memory network (LSTM) can be used to solve the problems with RNN.

What Is an RNN?

A recurrent neural network, a type of neural network, is used to process data that is sequential in nature, e.g., stock price data, text sentences, or sales of items.

Sequential data is a type of data where the value of data at timestep T depends upon the values of data at timesteps less than T. For instance, sound waves, text sentences, stock market price, etc. In the stock market price prediction problem, the value of the opening price of a stock at a given date depends upon the opening stock price of the previous days.

The difference between the architecture of a recurrent neural network and a simple neural network is presented in the following figure:

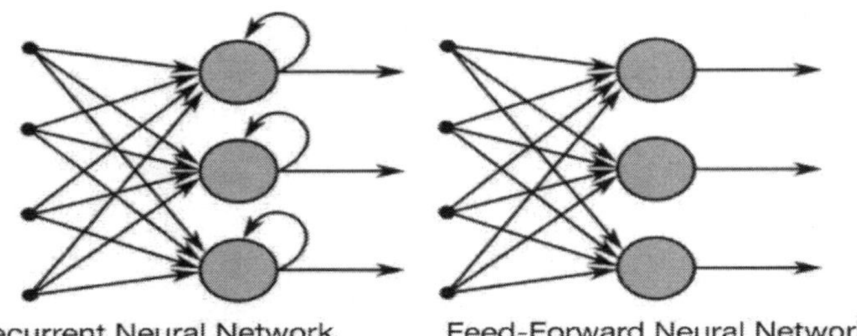

In a recurrent neural network, at each timestep, the previous output of the neuron is also multiplied by the current input via a weight vector. You can see from the above figure that the output from a neuron is looped back into for the next timestep. The following figure makes this concept further clear:

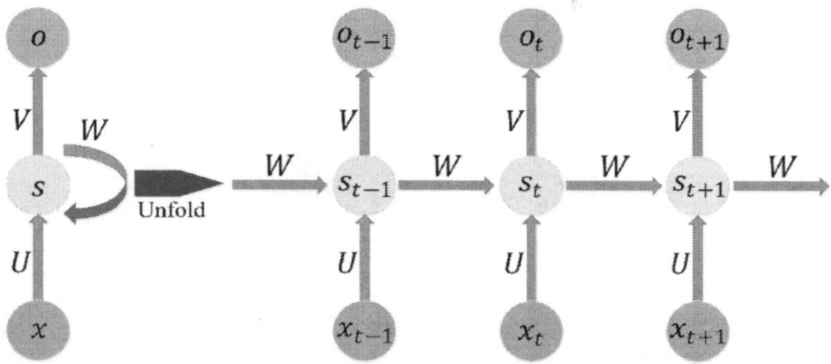

Here, we have a single neuron with one input and one output. On the right side, the process followed by a recurrent neural network is unfolded. You can see that at timestep t, the input is multiplied by weight vector U, while the previous output at time t−1, i.e., St−1 is multiplied by the weight vector W, the sum of the input vector XU + SW becomes the output at time T. This is how a recurrent neural network captures the sequential information.

Problems with RNN

A problem with the recurrent neural network is that while it can capture a shorter sequence, it tends to forget longer sequences.

For instance, it is easier to predict the missing word in the following sentence because the Keyword "Birds" is present in the same sentence.

"Birds fly in the ____."

RNN can easily guess that the missing word is "Clouds" here.

However, RNN cannot remember longer sequences such as the one ...

"Mike grew up in France. He likes to eat cheese, he plays piano....................................... .... and he speaks _______ fluently."

Here, the RNN can only guess that the missing word is "French" if it remembers the first sentence, i.e., "Mike grew up in France."

The recurrent neural networks consist of multiple recurrent layers, which results in a diminishing gradient problem. The diminishing gradient problem is that during backpropagation of the recurrent layer, the gradient of the earlier layer becomes infinitesimally small, which virtually makes the neural network initial layers stop from learning anything.

To solve this problem, a special type of recurrent neural network, i.e., Long Short-Term Memory (LSTM), has been developed.

What Is an LSTM?

LSTM is a type of RNN that is capable of remembering longer sequences, and, hence, it is one of the most frequently used RNNs for sequence tasks.

In LSTM, instead of a single unit in the recurrent cell, there are four interacting units, i.e., a forget gate, an input gate, an update gate, and an output gate. The overall architecture of an LSTM cell is shown in the following figure:

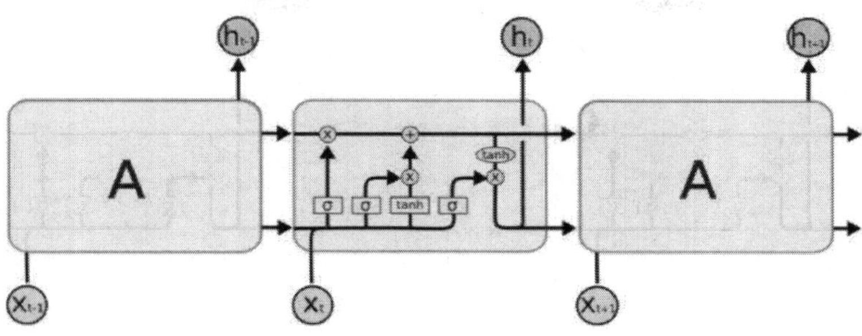

LSTM: Single Input - Single Output

Let's briefly discuss all the components of LSTM:

Cell State

The cell state in LSTM is responsible for remembering a long sequence. The following figure describes the cell state:

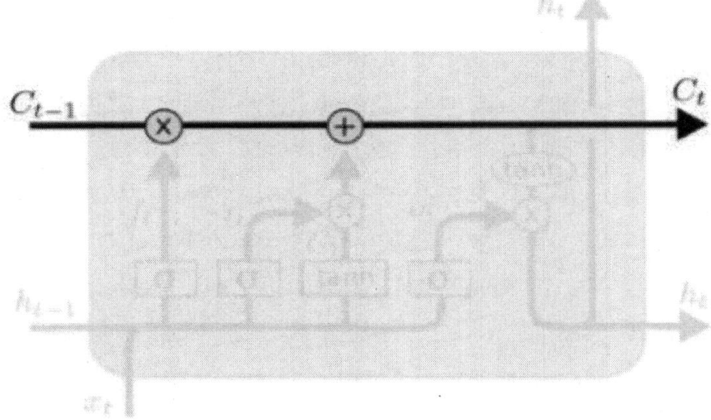

The cell state contains data from all the previous cells in the sequence. The LSTM is capable of adding or removing information to a cell state. In other words, LSTM tells the cell state which part of the previous information to remember and which information to forget.

Forget Gate

The forget gate basically tells the cell state which information to retain from the information in the previous step and which information to forget. The working and calculation formula for the forget gate is as follows:

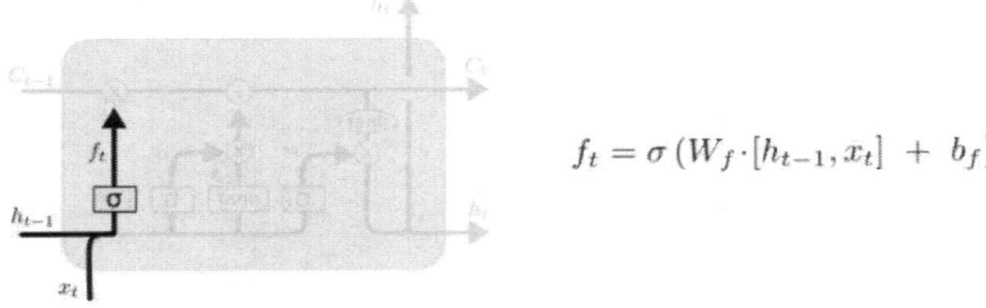

$$f_t = \sigma\left(W_f \cdot [h_{t-1}, x_t] \; + \; b_f\right)$$

Input Gate

The forget gate is used to decide which information to remember or forget. The input gate is responsible for updating or adding any new information in the cell state. Input gate has two parts: an input layer, which decides which part of the cell state is to be updated, and a tanh layer, which actually creates a vector of new values that are added or replaced in the cell state. The working of the input gate is explained in the following figure:

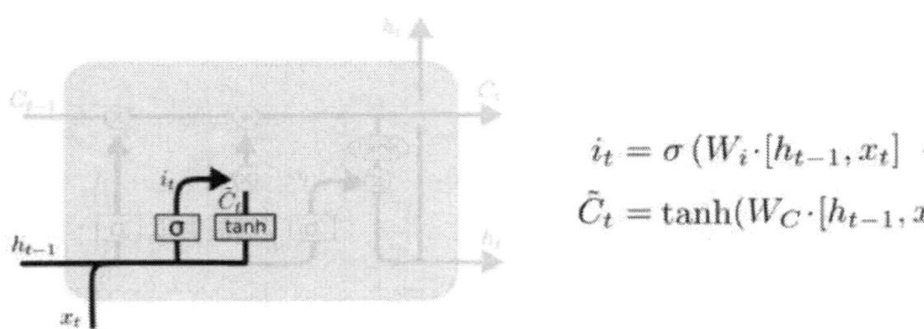

$$i_t = \sigma\left(W_i \cdot [h_{t-1}, x_t] \; + \; b_i\right)$$

$$\tilde{C}_t = \tanh(W_C \cdot [h_{t-1}, x_t] \; + \; b_C)$$

Update Gate

The forget gate tells us what to forget, and the input gate tells us what to add to the cell state. The next step is to actually perform these two operations. The update gate is basically used to perform these two operations. The functioning and the equations for the update gate are as follows:

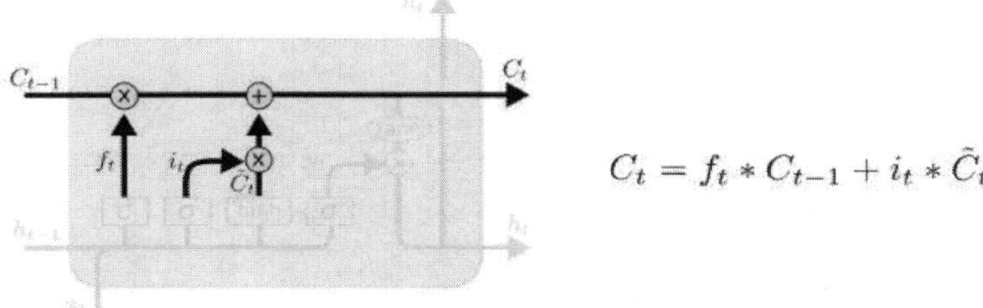

Output Gate

Finally, you have the output gate, which outputs the hidden state and the output just like a common recurrent neural network. The additional output from an LSTM node is the cell state, which runs between all the nodes in a sequence. The equations and the functioning of the output gate are depicted by the following figure:

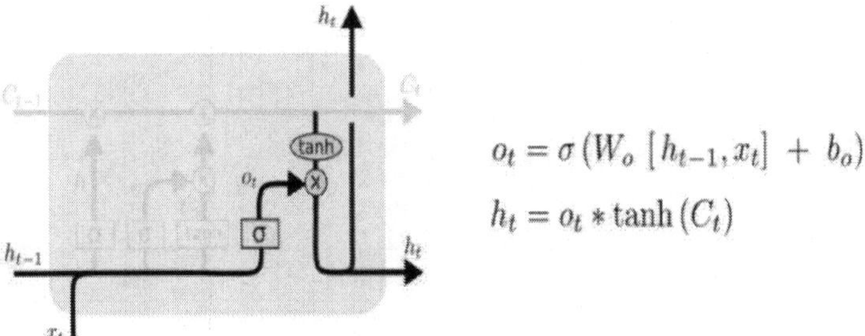

In the following sections, you will see how to use an LSTM for solving different types of sequence problems.

4.2. Predicting Future Stock Prices via LSTM in TensorFlow Keras

Stock price prediction is perhaps one of the most common applications of many to one or many to many sequence problems.

In this section, we will predict the opening stock price of the Facebook company, using the opening stock price of the previous 60 days. The training set consists of the stock price data of Facebook from 1st January 2015 to 31st December 2019, i.e., 5 years. The dataset can be downloaded from this site: https://finance.yahoo.com/quote/FB/history?p=FB.

The test data will consist of the opening stock prices of the Facebook company for the month of January 2020. The training file fb_train.csv and the test file fb_test.csv are also available in the *Data folder in the book resources*. Let's begin with the coding now.

4.2.1. Training the Stock Prediction Model

In this section, we will train our stock prediction model on the training set.

Before you train the stock market prediction model, upload the TensorFlow version by executing the following command on Google collaborator (https://colab.research.google.com/).

```
pip install --upgrade tensorflow
```

If your files are placed on Google drive, and you want to access them in Google Collaborator, to do so, you have to first mount the Google drive inside your Google Collaborator environment via the following script:

Script 1:

```
# mounting google drive
from google.colab import drive
drive.mount('/gdrive')
```

Next, to import the training dataset, execute the following script:

Script 2:

```
# importing libraries
import pandas as pd
import numpy as np

#importing dataset
fb_complete_data = pd.read_csv("/gdrive/My Drive/datasets/
fb_train.csv")
```

Running the following script will print the first five rows of the dataset.

Script 3:

```
#printing dataset header
fb_complete_data.head()
```

Output:

	Date	Open	High	Low	Close	Adj Close	Volume
0	2015-01-02	78.580002	78.930000	77.699997	78.449997	78.449997	18177500
1	2015-01-05	77.980003	79.250000	76.860001	77.190002	77.190002	26452200
2	2015-01-06	77.230003	77.589996	75.360001	76.150002	76.150002	27399300
3	2015-01-07	76.760002	77.360001	75.820000	76.150002	76.150002	22045300
4	2015-01-08	76.739998	78.230003	76.080002	78.180000	78.180000	23961000

The output shows that our dataset consists of seven columns. However, in this section, we are only interested in the Open column. Therefore, we will select the Open column from the dataset. Run the following script to do so.

Script 4:

```
#filtering open column
fb_training_processed = fb_complete_data[['Open']].values
```

Next, we will scale our dataset.

Script 5:

```
#scaling features
from sklearn.preprocessing import MinMaxScaler
scaler = MinMaxScaler(feature_range = (0, 1))

fb_training_scaled = scaler.fit_transform(fb_training_processed)
```

If you check the total length of the dataset, you will see it has 1,257 records, as shown below:

Script 6:

```
len(fb_training_scaled)
```

Output:

```
1257
```

Before we move forward, we need to divide our data into features and labels. Our feature set will consist of 60 timesteps of 1 feature. The feature set basically consists of the opening stock price of the past 60 days, while the label set will consist of the opening stock price of the 61st day. Based on the opening stock prices of the previous days, we will be able to predict the opening stock price for the next day.

Script 7:

```
#training features contained data of last 60 days
#training labels contain data of 61st day

fb_training_features= []
fb_training_labels = []
for i in range(60, len(fb_training_scaled)):
    fb_training_features.append(fb_training_scaled[i-60:i, 0])
    fb_training_labels.append(fb_training_scaled[i, 0])
```

We need to convert our data into a Numpy array before we can use it as input with Keras. The following script does that:

Script 8:

```
#converting training data to numpy arrays
X_train = np.array(fb_training_features)
y_train = np.array(fb_training_labels)
```

Let's print the shape of our dataset.

Script 9:

```
print(X_train.shape)
print(y_train.shape)
```

Output:

```
(1197, 60)
(1197,)
```

We need to reshape our input features into a three-dimensional format.

Script 10:

```
converting data into 3D shape
X_train = np.reshape(X_train, (X_train.shape[0], X_train.shape[1], 1))
```

The following script creates our LSTM model. We have four LSTM layers with 100 nodes each. Each LSTM layer is followed by a dropout layer to avoid overfitting. The final dense layer has one node since the output is a single value.

Script 11:

```
#importing libraries
import numpy as np
import matplotlib.pyplot as plt
from tensorflow.keras.layers import Input, Activation, Dense, Flatten, Dropout,  Flatten, LSTM
from tensorflow.keras.models import Model
```

Script 12:

```
#defining the LSTM network

input_layer = Input(shape = (X_train.shape[1], 1))
lstm1 = LSTM(100, activation='relu', return_sequences=True)(input_layer)
do1 = Dropout(0.2)(lstm1)
lstm2 = LSTM(100, activation='relu', return_sequences=True)(do1)
do2 = Dropout(0.2)(lstm2)
lstm3 = LSTM(100, activation='relu', return_sequences=True)(do2)
do3 = Dropout(0.2)(lstm3)
lstm4 = LSTM(100, activation='relu')(do3)
do4 = Dropout(0.2)(lstm4)

output_layer = Dense(1)(do4)
model = Model(input_layer, output_layer)
model.compile(optimizer='adam', loss='mse')
```

Next, we need to convert the output y into a column vector.

Script 13:

```
print(X_train.shape)
print(y_train.shape)
y_train= y_train.reshape(-1,1)
print(y_train.shape)
```

Output:

```
(1197, 60, 1)
(1197,)
(1197, 1)
```

The following script trains our stock price prediction model on the training set.

Script 14:

```
#training the model
model_history = model.fit(X_train, y_train, epochs=100, verbose=1, batch_size = 32)
```

You can see the results for the last five epochs in the output.

Output:

```
Epoch 96/100
38/38 [==============================] - 11s 299ms/step -
loss: 0.0018
Epoch 97/100
38/38 [==============================] - 11s 294ms/step -
loss: 0.0019
Epoch 98/100
38/38 [==============================] - 11s 299ms/step -
loss: 0.0018
Epoch 99/100
38/38 [==============================] - 12s 304ms/step -
loss: 0.0018
Epoch 100/100
38/38 [==============================] - 11s 299ms/step -
loss: 0.0021
```

Our model has been trained; next, we will test our stock prediction model on the test data.

4.2.2. Testing the Stock Prediction Model

The test data should also be converted into the right shape to test our stock prediction model. We will do that later. Let's first import the data and then remove all the columns from the test data except the **Open** column.

Script 15:

```
#creating test set
fb_testing_complete_data = pd.read_csv("/gdrive/My Drive/datasets/fb_test.csv")
fb_testing_processed = fb_testing_complete_data[['Open']].values
```

Let's concatenate the training and test sets. We do this because to predict the first value in the test set, the input will be the data from the past 60 days, which is basically the data from the last 60 days in the training set.

Script 16:

```
fb_all_data = pd.concat((fb_complete_data['Open'], fb_testing_complete_data['Open']), axis=0)
```

The following script creates our final input feature set.

Script 17:

```
test_inputs = fb_all_data [len(fb_all_data) - len(fb_testing_complete_data) - 60:].values
print(test_inputs.shape)
```

You can see that the length of the input data is 80. Here, the first 60 records are the last 60 records from the training data, and the last 20 records are the 20 records from the test file.

Output:

```
(80,)
```

We need to scale our data and convert it into a column vector.

Script 18:

```
test_inputs = test_inputs.reshape(-1,1)
test_inputs = scaler.transform(test_inputs)
print(test_inputs.shape)
```

Output:

```
(80, 1)
```

As we did with the training data, we need to divide our input data into features and labels. Here is the script that does that.

Script 19:

```
fb_test_features = []
for i in range(60, 80):
    fb_test_features.append(test_inputs[i-60:i, 0])
```

Let's now print our feature set.

Script 20:

```
X_test = np.array(fb_test_features)
print(X_test.shape)
```

Output:

```
(20, 60)
```

Our feature set is currently 2-dimensional. But the LSTM algorithm in Keras accepts data in 3-dimensional. The following script converts our input features into a 3-dimensional shape.

Script 21:

```
#converting test data into 3D shape
X_test = np.reshape(X_test, (X_test.shape[0], X_test.
shape[1], 1))
print(X_test.shape)
```

Output:

```
(20, 60, 1)
```

Now is the time to make predictions on the test set. The following script does that:

Script 22:

```
#making predictions on test set
y_pred =  model.predict(X_test)
```

Since we scaled our input feature, we need to apply the **inverse_transform()** method of the **scaler** object on the predicted output to get the original output values.

Script 23:

```
#converting scaled data back to original data
y_pred = scaler.inverse_transform(y_pred)
```

Finally, to compare the predicted output with the actual stock price values, you can plot the two values via the following script:

Script 24:

```
#plotting original and predicted stock values
plt.figure(figsize=(8,6))
plt.plot(fb_testing_processed, color='red', label='Actual Facebook Stock Price')
plt.plot(y_pred , color='green', label='Predicted Facebook Stock Price')
plt.title('Facebook Stock Prices')
plt.xlabel('Date')
plt.ylabel('Stock Price')
plt.legend()
plt.show()
```

Output:

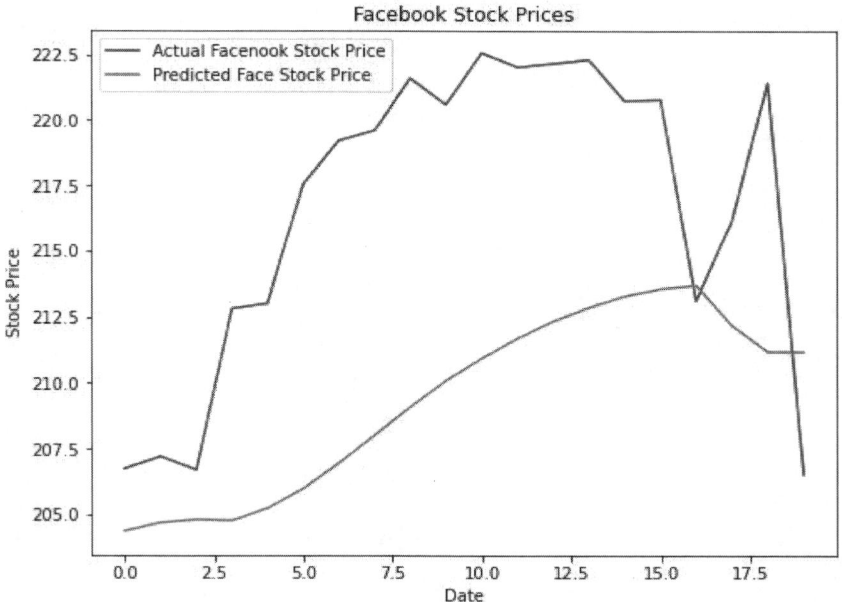

The output shows that our algorithm has been able to partially capture the trend of the future opening stock prices for Facebook data.

Exercise 4.1

Question 1:

The shape of the feature set passed to the LSTM's input layer should be:

A. Number of Records, Features, Timesteps

B. Timesteps, Features, Number of Records

C. Features, Timesteps, Number of Records

D. Number of Records, Timesteps, Features

Question 2:

RNN is not capable of learning longer sequences because of:

A. Exploding Gradient

B. Diminishing Gradient

C. Low Gradient

D. None of the above

Question 3:

An RNN is useful when the data is in the form of:

A. A table with unrelated records

B. An image with spatial information

C. A sequence with related records

D. None of the above

PROJECT

5

Language Translation Using Seq2Seq Encoder-Decoder LSTM

In project 4 of this book, you saw how an LSTM can be used for predicting stock prices. In this project, you will see how a combination of two LSTM networks can be used to create models capable of translating sentences from one language to another.

Seq2seq models are based on encoder-decoder architecture, which learns the mapping between input and output sentences of varying lengths. Seq2seq models can be used to develop chatbots, text translation, question-answering machines, etc.

In this project, you will see an application of the Seq2Seq model for text translation. So, let's begin with much ado.

5.1. Creating Seq2Seq Training Model for Language Translation

A Seq2seq model typically consists of two models. In the training phase, the encoder receives an input sentence and feeds it to the decoder. The decoder then predicts the output or translated sentence in our case. Both encoder and decoders are connected LSTM networks. The process is shown in the following figure. Here, the offset tag for decoder input is "<s>", and the offset tag for decoder output is </s>.

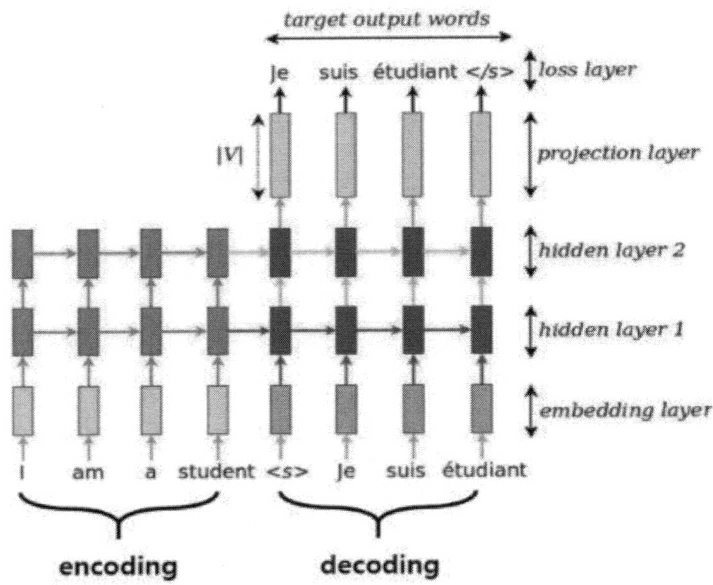

The input to the encoder is the sentence in the original language, which is English in the above example. The output of the encoder is the hidden and cell states. The input to the decoder is the hidden and cell states from the encoder plus the target dataset, one step offset.

For instance, if you look at the decoder input, in the first step, the input is always <s>. The decoder output at the first timestep is the ground truth translated output word. For instance, the first output word is "Je" in the above example. In the second step, the input to the decoder is the hidden and cell states from the previous step plus the first actual word in the output sentence, i.e., "Je." This process where the ground truth value of the previous output is fed as input to the next timestep is called teacher forcing. All the sentences are ended with an end of sentence token to stop the decoder from making predictions when an end of sentence tag is encountered, which is </s> in the above diagram.

Let's code the above training model. The first step, as always, is to import the libraries.

Script 1:

```
import os, sys

from keras.models import Model
from keras.layers import Input, LSTM, GRU, Dense, Embedding
from keras.preprocessing.text import Tokenizer
from keras.preprocessing.sequence import pad_sequences
from keras.utils import to_categorical
import numpy as np
import matplotlib.pyplot as plt
```

Next, we need to define a few configurations for our LSTM based encoder and decoder models, as well as for the word2vec based embedding layers.

Script 2:

```
BATCH_SIZE = 64
NUM_EPOCHS = 20
LSTM_NODES =512
TOTAL_SENTENCES = 20000
MAX_SEN_LENGTH = 50
MAX_NUM_WORDS = 20000
EMBEDDING_SIZE = 100
```

Since the script in this project is run using Google Collaboratory, the datasets are uploaded to Google Drive and then imported into the application. To import datasets from Google drive to Google Collaboratory, run the following script:

Script 3:

```
from google.colab import drive
drive.mount('/gdrive')
```

The dataset that we are going to use for training our seq2seq model is available freely at this link: http://www.manythings.org/anki/.

Go to the link and then download the *fra-eng.zip* file. Unzip the file, and you should see the *fra.txt* file. This file contains our dataset. The dataset is also available by the name: *fra.txt* in the *Data folder in the book resources*. The first 10 lines of the file look like this:

```
Go. Va !    CC-BY 2.0 (France) Attribution: tatoeba.org #2877272 (CM) & #1158250 (Wittydev)
Hi. Salut ! CC-BY 2.0 (France) Attribution: tatoeba.org #538123 (CM) & #509819 (Aiji)
Hi. Salut.  CC-BY 2.0 (France) Attribution: tatoeba.org #538123 (CM) & #4320462 (gillux)
Run!    Cours ! CC-BY 2.0 (France) Attribution: tatoeba.org #906328 (papabear) & #906331 (sacredceltic)
Run!    Courez !    CC-BY 2.0 (France) Attribution: tatoeba.org #906328 (papabear) & #906332 (sacredceltic)
Who?    Qui ?   CC-BY 2.0 (France) Attribution: tatoeba.org #2083030 (CK) & #4366796 (gillux)
Wow!    ? a alors !  CC-BY 2.0 (France) Attribution: tatoeba.org #52027 (Zifre) & #374631 (zmoo)
Fire!   Au feu !    CC-BY 2.0 (France) Attribution: tatoeba.org #1829639 (Spamster) & #4627939 (sacredceltic)
Help!   ? l'aide !  CC-BY 2.0 (France) Attribution: tatoeba.org #435084 (lukaszpp) & #128430 (sysko)
Jump.   Saute.  CC-BY 2.0 (France) Attribution: tatoeba.org #631038 (Shishir) & #2416938 (Phoenix)
```

Each line in the *fra.txt* file contains a sentence in English, followed by a tab and then the translation of the English sentence in French, again a tab, and then the attribute.

We are only interested in the English and French sentences. The following script creates three lists. The first list contains all the English sentences, which serve as encoder input.

The second list contains the decoder input sentences in French, where the offset <sos> is prefixed before all the sentences.

Finally, the third list contains decoder outputs where <eos> is appended at the end of each sentence in French.

Script 4:

```
input_english_sentences = []
output_french_sentences = []
output_french_sentences_inputs = []
count = 0
for line in open(r'/gdrive/My Drive/datasets/fra.txt', encoding="utf-8"):
    count += 1
    if count > TOTAL_SENTENCES:
        break
    if '\t' not in line:
        continue
    input_sentence = line.rstrip().split('\t')[0]
    output = line.rstrip().split('\t')[1]
    output_sentence = output + ' <eos>'
    output_sentence_input = '<sos> ' + output
    input_english_sentences.append(input_sentence)
    output_french_sentences.append(output_sentence)
    output_french_sentences_inputs.append(output_sentence_input)
```

Let's see how many total English and French sentences we have in our dataset:

Script 5:

```
print("sentences in input:", len(input_english_sentences))
print("sentences in output:", len(output_french_sentences))
print("sentences for output input:", len(output_french_sentences_inputs))
```

Output:

```
Sentences in input: 20000
Sentences in output: 20000
Sentences for output input: 20000
```

Let's randomly print a sentence in English and its French translation (both the decoder input and the decoder output).

Script 6:

```
print(input_english_sentences[175])
print(output_french_sentences[175])
print(output_french_sentences_inputs[175])
```

Output:

```
I'm shy.
Je suis timide. <eos>
<sos> Je suis timide.
```

You can see that the sentence at index 175 is "I'm shy." In the decoder input, the translated sentence contains <sos> tag at the beginning, while the output contains an <eos> tag.

Next, we need to tokenize both the input English sentences. This is a mandatory step before word embeddings.

Script 7:

```
input_eng_tokenizer = Tokenizer(num_words=MAX_NUM_WORDS)
input_eng_tokenizer.fit_on_texts(input_english_sentences)
input_eng_integer_seq = input_eng_tokenizer.texts_to_sequences(input_english_sentences)

word2idx_eng_inputs = input_eng_tokenizer.word_index
print('Sum of unique words in English sentences: %s' % len(word2idx_eng_inputs))

max_input_len = max(len(sen) for sen in input_eng_integer_seq)
print("Length of longest sentence in English sentences: %g" % max_input_len)
```

Output:

```
Sum of unique words in English sentences: 3514
Length of longest sentence in English sentences: 6
```

Similarly, the following script tokenizes the output French sentences.

Script 8:

```
output_french_tokenizer = Tokenizer(num_words=MAX_NUM_WORDS, filters='')
output_french_tokenizer.fit_on_texts(output_french_sentences + output_french_sentences_inputs)
output_french_integer_seq = output_french_tokenizer.texts_to_sequences(output_french_sentences)
output_input_french_integer_seq = output_french_tokenizer.texts_to_sequences(output_french_sentences_inputs)

word2idx_french_outputs = output_french_tokenizer.word_index
print('Sum of unique words in French sentences: %s' % len(word2idx_french_outputs))

num_words_output = len(word2idx_french_outputs) + 1
```

```
max_out_len = max(len(sen) for sen in output_french_integer_seq)
print("Length of longest sentence in French sentences: %g" % max_out_len)
```

Output:

```
Sum of unique words in French sentences: 9532
Length of longest sentence in French sentences: 13
```

Next, we need to pad our input and output sequences so that they can have the same length. The following script applies padding to the input sequences for the encoder.

Script 9:

```
encoder_input_eng_sequences = pad_sequences(input_eng_integer_seq, maxlen=max_input_len)
print("encoder_input_eng_sequences.shape:", encoder_input_eng_sequences.shape)
print("encoder_input_eng_sequences[175]:", encoder_input_eng_sequences[175])

print(word2idx_eng_inputs["i'm"])
print(word2idx_eng_inputs["shy"])
```

Since the maximum length of an English sentence is 6, you can see that the shape of the encoder input sentence is (20000, 6), which means that all sentences have now become of equal length of 6. For instance, if you print the padded version for the sentence at index 175, you see [0, 0, 0, 0, 6, 307]. Since the actual sentence is "I'm shy," we can print the index for these words and see the indexes (6, 37) match the indexes in the padded sequence for the sentence at index 175.

Output:

```
encoder_input_eng_sequences.shape: (20000, 6)
encoder_input_eng_sequences[175]: [  0   0   0   0   6 307]
6
307
```

Similarly, the following script applies padding to the decoder input French sentences.

Script 10:

```
decoder_input_french_sequences = pad_sequences(output_input_french_integer_seq, maxlen=max_out_len, padding='post')
print("decoder_input_french_sequences.shape:", decoder_input_french_sequences.shape)
print("decoder_input_french_sequences[175]:", decoder_input_french_sequences[175])

print(word2idx_french_outputs["<sos>"])
print(word2idx_french_outputs["je"])
print(word2idx_french_outputs["suis"])
print(word2idx_french_outputs["timide."])
```

Output:

```
decoder_input_french_sequences.shape: (20000, 13)
decoder_input_french_sequences[175]: [  2   3   6 339   0   0
   0   0   0   0   0   0   0]
2
3
6
339
```

And the following script applies padding to the decoder output French sentences.

Script 11:

```
decoder_output_french_sequences = pad_sequences(output_french_integer_seq, maxlen=max_out_len, padding='post')
```

The next step is to create word embeddings for the input and output sentences. Word embeddings are used to convert a word into numerical vectors since deep learning algorithms work with numbers only. For the input sentences, we can use the Glove word embeddings since the sentences are English. You can download the Glove word embeddings from Stanford Glove (https://stanford.io/2MJW98X).

We will see how to load Stanford Glove 100-dimensional pre-trained word embeddings into our application. To do so, you need to download the *glove.6B.100d.txt* from the Stanford Glove online source (https://stanford.io/2MJW98X).

The following scripts create the embedding dictionary for the Glove word vectors.

Script 12:

```
from numpy import array
from numpy import asarray
from numpy import zeros

embeddings_dictionary = dict()

glove_file = open(r'/gdrive/My Drive/datasets/glove.6B.100d.txt', encoding="utf8")

for line in glove_file:
    records = line.split()
    word = records[0]
    vector_dimensions = asarray(records[1:], dtype='float32')
    embeddings_dictionary[word] = vector_dimensions
glove_file.close()
```

And the following script creates an embedding matrix that will be used in the embedding layer to the encoder LSTM.

Script 13:

```
num_words = min(MAX_NUM_WORDS, len(word2idx_eng_inputs) + 1)
embedding_matrix = zeros((num_words, EMBEDDING_SIZE))
for word, index in word2idx_eng_inputs.items():
    embedding_vector = embeddings_dictionary.get(word)
    if embedding_vector is not None:
        embedding_matrix[index] = embedding_vector
```

The following script creates an embedding layer for the encoder LSTM.

Script 14:

```
embedding_layer = Embedding(num_words, EMBEDDING_SIZE,
weights=[embedding_matrix], input_length=max_input_len)
```

The next step is to create the decoder embedding layer. The first step is to create an empty embedding matrix of the shape (number of the output sentence, length of the longest sentence in the output, total number of unique words in the output). The following script does that.

Script 15:

```
decoder_one_hot_targets = np.zeros((
        len(input_english_sentences),
        max_out_len,
        num_words_output
    ),
    dtype='float32'
)
```

Script 16:

```
decoder_one_hot_targets.shape
```

Output:

```
(20000, 13, 9533)
```

The next step is to add one at those indexes in the decoder embedding matrix where a word exists in the original decoder input and output sequences.

Script 17:

```
for i, d in enumerate(decoder_output_french_sequences):
    for t, word in enumerate(d):
        decoder_one_hot_targets[i, t, word] = 1
```

The following script creates the encoder model.

Script 18:

```
encoder_inputs_eng_placeholder = Input(shape=(max_input_len,))
x = embedding_layer(encoder_inputs_eng_placeholder)
encoder = LSTM(LSTM_NODES, return_state=True)

encoder_outputs, h, c = encoder(x)
encoder_states = [h, c]
```

And the following script creates the decoder model. You can see that in the decoder model, a custom embedding layer is being used.

Script 19:

```
decoder_inputs_french_placeholder = Input(shape=(max_out_len,))

decoder_embedding = Embedding(num_words_output, LSTM_NODES)
decoder_inputs_x = decoder_embedding(decoder_inputs_french_placeholder)

decoder_lstm = LSTM(LSTM_NODES, return_sequences=True, return_state=True)
decoder_outputs, _, _ = decoder_lstm(decoder_inputs_x, initial_state=encoder_states)

```

```
###

decoder_dense = Dense(num_words_output,
activation='softmax')
decoder_outputs = decoder_dense(decoder_outputs)
```

The following script creates the complete training model for our seq2seq model.

Script 20:

```
model = Model([encoder_inputs_eng_placeholder,
  decoder_inputs_french_placeholder], decoder_outputs)
model.compile(
    optimizer='rmsprop',
    loss='categorical_crossentropy',
    metrics=['accuracy']
)
```

Execute the following script to display the training model.

Script 21:

```
from keras.utils import plot_model
plot_model(model, to_file='model_plot4a.png', show_
shapes=True, show_layer_names=True)
```

Output:

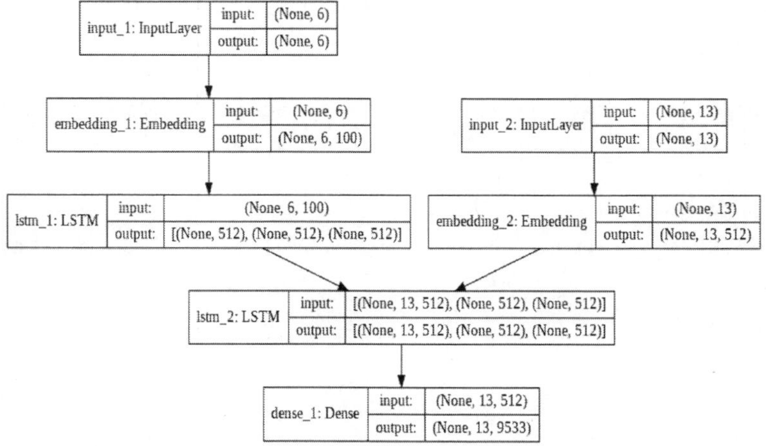

Finally, the following script trains the model.

Script 22:

```
r = model.fit(
    [encoder_input_eng_sequences, decoder_input_french_sequences],
    decoder_one_hot_targets,
    batch_size=BATCH_SIZE,
    epochs=NUM_EPOCHS,
    validation_split=0.1,
)
```

At the end of 20 epochs, an accuracy of around 79.67 is achieved.

Output:

```
Epoch 16/20
18000/18000 [==============================] - 23s 1ms/step
- loss: 0.4830 - accuracy: 0.9182 - val_loss: 1.4919 - val_
accuracy: 0.7976
Epoch 17/20
18000/18000 [==============================] - 23s 1ms/step
- loss: 0.4730 - accuracy: 0.9202 - val_loss: 1.5083 - val_
accuracy: 0.7962
Epoch 18/20
18000/18000 [==============================] - 23s 1ms/step
- loss: 0.4616 - accuracy: 0.9219 - val_loss: 1.5127 - val_
accuracy: 0.7963
Epoch 19/20
18000/18000 [==============================] - 22s 1ms/step
- loss: 0.4515 - accuracy: 0.9235 - val_loss: 1.5249 - val_
accuracy: 0.7963
Epoch 20/20
18000/18000 [==============================] - 23s 1ms/step
- loss: 0.4407 - accuracy: 0.9250 - val_loss: 1.5303 - val_
accuracy: 0.7967
```

5.2. Making Predictions Using Seq2Seq

You saw how to train a model in the previous section. In this section, you will see how to make predictions. The process of making predictions is elaborated in the following figure.

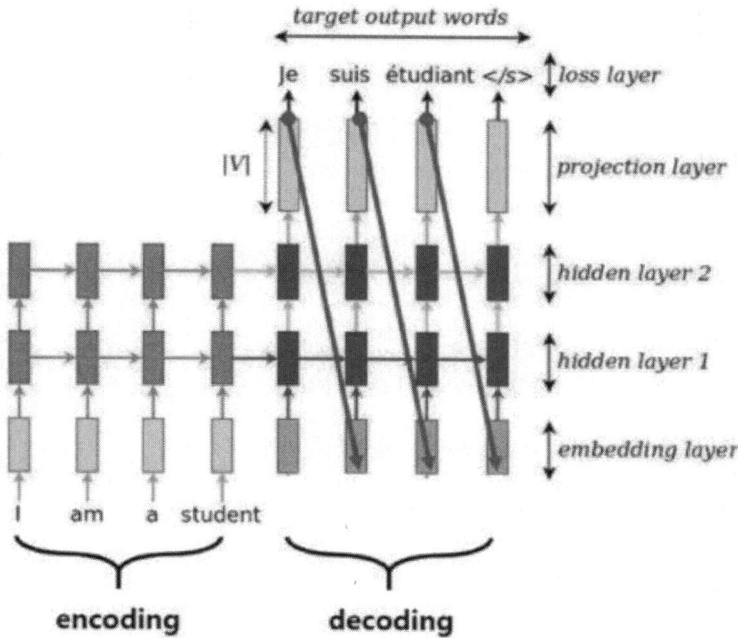

In the prediction phase, the input to the encoder is a complete sentence in its original language, just like the encoder. However, one of the inputs to the decoder is the hidden and cell states from the encoder. And unlike the training phase, where the whole target sentence is fed as input simultaneously, during prediction at the first step, the word <sos> is fed as decoder input. On the basis of the hidden and cell states and the first word <sos>, the decoder makes a prediction for the first translated word, which is "suis" in the above figure.

At the second timestep, the input to the decoder is the hidden state and cell state from the first decoder timestep, and the output from the first decoder timestep, which is "Je." The process continues until the decoder predicts <eos>, which corresponds to the end of the sentence.

The following script implements the model for making predictions for translating text from English to French using the seq2seq model.

Script 23:

```
encoder_prediction_model = Model(encoder_inputs_eng_placeholder, encoder_states)

decoder_state_input_h = Input(shape=(LSTM_NODES,))
decoder_state_input_c = Input(shape=(LSTM_NODES,))
decoder_states_inputs = [decoder_state_input_h, decoder_state_input_c]

decoder_inputs_single = Input(shape=(1,))
decoder_inputs_single_x = decoder_embedding(decoder_inputs_single)

decoder_outputs, h, c = decoder_lstm(decoder_inputs_single_x, initial_state=decoder_states_inputs)

decoder_states = [h, c]
decoder_outputs = decoder_dense(decoder_outputs)

decoder_model = Model(
    [decoder_inputs_single] + decoder_states_inputs,
    [decoder_outputs] + decoder_states
)
```

The prediction model is plotted via the following script:

Script 24:

```
from keras.utils import plot_model
plot_model(model, to_file='model_plot4a.png', show_
shapes=True, show_layer_names=True)
```

Output:

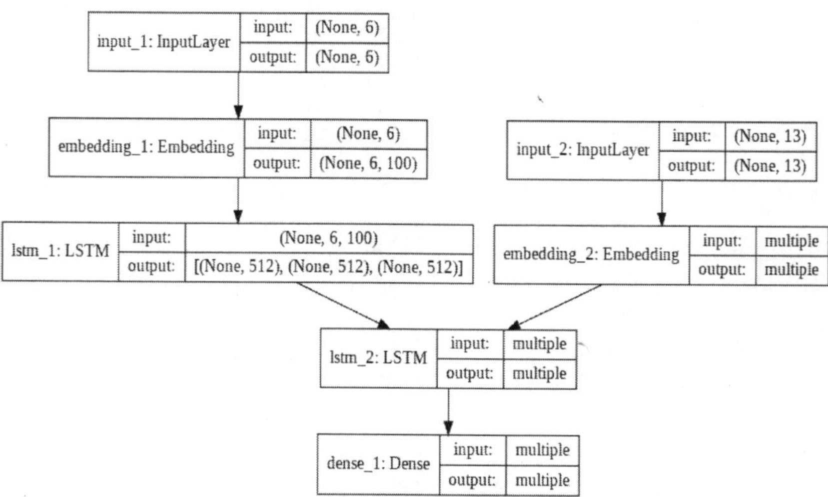

The prediction model makes predictions in the form of integers. You will need to convert the integers back to text. The following script creates an index to word dictionaries for both the input and output sentences.

Script 25:

```
idx2word_eng_input = {v:k for k, v in word2idx_eng_inputs.
items()}
idx2word_french_target = {v:k for k, v in word2idx_french_
outputs.items()}
```

In the following script, we create a **"perform_translation()"** method which accepts an input sequence of a sentence. The encoder encodes the input sequence and passes the hidden state and the cell state to the decoder. The first input to the decoder is the "sos" tag along with hidden and cell states from the encoder. A loop runs for the maximum sentence length time. During each iteration, a prediction is made. If the predicted word is "<eos>", the loop terminates. Else, using the predicted index, the actual word is found from the index to the word dictionary, and the word is appended to the output sentence. The index and the hidden state and cell states of the decoder are updated, and the new values are used to make predictions using the decoder model again. The following script contains the code logic for the **"perform_translation()"** function.

Script 26:

```
def perform_translation(input_seq):
  states_value = encoder_prediction_model.predict(input_seq)
    target_seq = np.zeros((1, 1))
    target_seq[0, 0] = word2idx_french_outputs['<sos>']
    eos = word2idx_french_outputs['<eos>']
    output_sentence = []

    for _ in range(max_out_len):
        output_tokens, h, c = decoder_model.predict([target_seq] + states_value)
        idx = np.argmax(output_tokens[0, 0, :])

        if eos == idx:
            break

        word = ''

        if idx > 0:
            word = idx2word_french_target[idx]
            output_sentence.append(word)

        target_seq[0, 0] = idx
        states_value = [h, c]

    return ' '.join(output_sentence)
```

Now is the time to make predictions. The following script randomly chooses an input sentence from the list of input sentence sequences. The sentence sequence is passed to the **"perform_translation()"** method, which returns the translated sentence in French.

Script 27:

```
random_sentence_index = np.random.choice(len(input_english_sentences))
input_eng_seq = encoder_input_eng_sequences[random_sentence_index:random_sentence_index+1]
translation = perform_translation(input_eng_seq)
print('-')
print('Input Sentence:', input_english_sentences[random_sentence_index])
print('Translated Sentence:', translation)
```

The output shows that the sentence chosen randomly by our script is "You need sleep," which has been successfully translated into "vous avez besoin de sommeil" in French.

Output:

```
Input Sentence: You need sleep.
Translated Sentence: vous avez besoin de sommeil.
```

Further Readings – Seq2Seq Modeling

To study more about word seq2seq modeling, see these resources:

https://bit.ly/2Y8L9Zn

https://bit.ly/2ZkvmWI

Exercise 5.1

Question 1:

This process where the ground truth value of the previous output is fed as input to the next timestep is called teacher forcing:

A. Truth Labeling

B. Input Labeling

C. Input Forcing

D. Teacher Forcing

Question 2:

In the seq2seq model, the input to the node in the decoder layer is:

A. Hidden state from the encoder

B. Cell state from the encoder

C. A "start of sentence" tag

D. All of the above

Question 3:

To end predictions using decoder LSTM in seq2seq, what strategy is adopted?

A. End sentence if maximum sentence length is achieved

B. End sentence if "end of sentence" tag is predicted

C. Both A and B

D. None of the above

PROJECT

6

Classifying Cats and Dogs Images Using Convolutional Neural Networks

In the previous three projects, you studied different feedforward densely connected neural networks and recurrent neural networks. In this project, you will study the Convolutional Neural Network (CNN).

You will see how you can use convolutional neural networks (CNN) to classify cats' and dogs' images. Before you see the actual code, let's first briefly discuss what convolutional neural networks are.

What Is a Convolutional Neural Network?

A convolutional neural network, a type of neural network, is used to classify spatial data, for instance, images, sequences, etc. In an image, each pixel is somehow related to some other pictures. Looking at a single pixel, you cannot guess the image. Rather, you have to look at the complete picture to guess the image. A CNN does exactly that. Using a kernel or feature detects, it detects features within an image.

A combination of these images then forms the complete image, which can then be classified using a densely connected neural network. The steps involved in a Convolutional Neural Network have been explained in the next section.

6.1. How CNN Classifies Images?

Before we actually implement a CNN with TensorFlow Keras library for cats and dogs' image classification, let's briefly see how a CNN classifies images.

How Do Computers See Images?

When humans see an image, they see lines, circles, squares, and different shapes. However, a computer sees an image differently. For a computer, an image is no more than a 2-D set of pixels arranged in a certain manner. For greyscale images, the pixel value can be between 0–255, while for color images, there are three channels: red, green, and blue. Each channel can have a pixel value between 0–255.

Look at the following image 6.1.

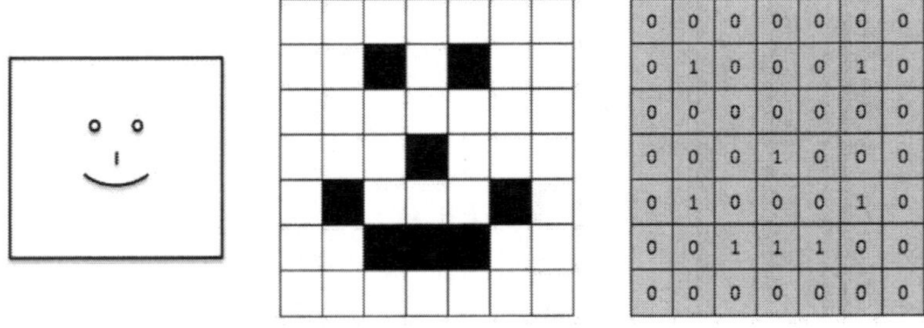

Image 6.1: How do computers see images?

Here, the box on the leftmost is what humans see. They see a smiling face. However, a computer sees it in the form of pixel values of 0s and 1s, as shown on the right-hand side. Here, 0 indicates a white pixel, whereas 1 indicates a black pixel. In the real world, 1 indicates a white pixel, while 0 indicates a black pixel.

Now, we know how a computer sees images, the next step is to explain the steps involved in the image classification using a convolutional neural network.

The following are the steps involved in image classification with CNN:

1. The Convolution Operation
2. The ReLu Operation
3. The Pooling Operation
4. Flattening and Fully Connected Layer

The Convolution Operation

The convolution operation is the first step involved in the image classification with a convolutional neural network.

In convolution operation, you have an image and a feature detector. The values of the feature detector are initialized randomly. The feature detector is moved over the image from left to right. The values in the feature detector are multiplied by the corresponding values in the image, and then all the values in the feature detector are added. The resultant value is added to the feature map.

Look at the following image, for example:

0	0	0	0	0	0	0
0	1	0	0	0	1	0
0	0	0	0	0	0	0
0	0	0	1	0	0	0
0	1	0	0	0	1	0
0	0	1	1	1	0	0
0	0	0	0	0	0	0

Input Image

⊗

0	0	1
1	0	0
0	1	1

Feature Detector

=

0	1	0	0	0
0	1	1	1	0
1	0	1	2	1
1	4	2	1	0
0	0	1	2	1

Feature Map

In the above figure, we have an input image of 7 x 7. The feature detector is of size 3 x 3. The feature detector is placed over the image at the top left of the input image, and then the pixel values in the feature detector are multiplied by the pixel values in the input image. The result is then added. The feature detector then moves to the N step toward the right. Here, N refers to stride. A stride is basically the number of steps that a feature detector takes from left to right and then from top to bottom to find a new value for the feature map.

In reality, there are multiple feature detectors, as shown in the following image:

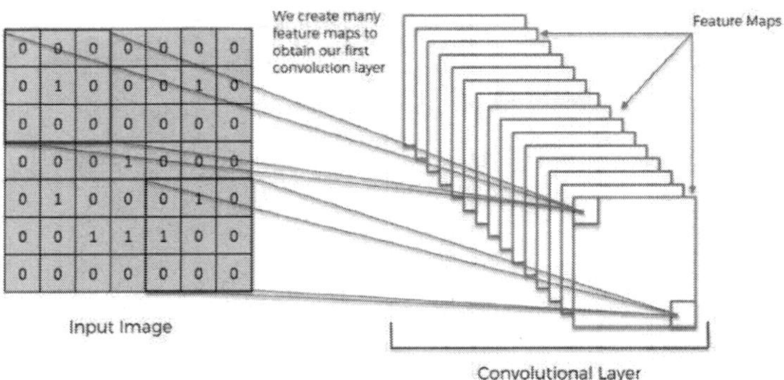

Each feature detector is responsible for detecting a particular feature in the image.

The ReLu Operation

In the ReLu operation, you simply apply the ReLu activation function on the feature map generated as a result of the convolution operation. Convolution operation gives us linear values. The ReLu operation is performed to introduce non-linearity in the image.

In the ReLu operation, all the negative values in a feature map are replaced by 0. All the positive values are left untouched.

Suppose we have the following feature map:

−4	2	1	−2
1	−1	8	0
3	−3	1	4
1	0	1	−2

When the ReLu function is applied on the feature map, the resultant feature map looks like this:

0	2	1	0
1	−0	8	0
3	0	1	4
1	0	1	0

The Pooling Operation

Pooling operation is performed in order to introduce spatial invariance in the feature map. Pooling operation is performed after convolution and ReLu operations.

Let's first understand what spatial invariance is. If you look at the following three images, you can easily identify that these images contain cheetahs.

The second image is disoriented, and the third image is distorted. However, we are still able to identify that all three images contain cheetahs based on certain features.

Pooling does exactly that. In pooling, we have a feature map and then a pooling filter, which can be of any size. Next, we move the pooling filter over the feature map and apply the pooling operation. There can be many pooling operations, such as max pooling, min pooling, and average pooling. In max pooling, we choose the maximum value from the pooling filter. Pooling not only introduces spatial invariance but also reduces the size of an image.

Look at the following image. Here, in the 3rd and 4th rows and 1st and 2nd columns, we have four values 1, 0, 1, and 4. When we apply max pooling on these four pixels, the maximum value will be chosen, i.e., you can see 4 in the pooled feature map.

0	1	0	0	0
0	1	1	1	0
1	0	1	2	1
1	4	2	1	0
0	0	1	2	1

Feature Map

Max Pooling

1	1	0
4	2	1
0	2	1

Pooled Feature Map

Flattening and Fully Connected Layer

For finding more features from an image, the pooled feature maps are flattened to form a one-dimensional vector, as shown in the following figure:

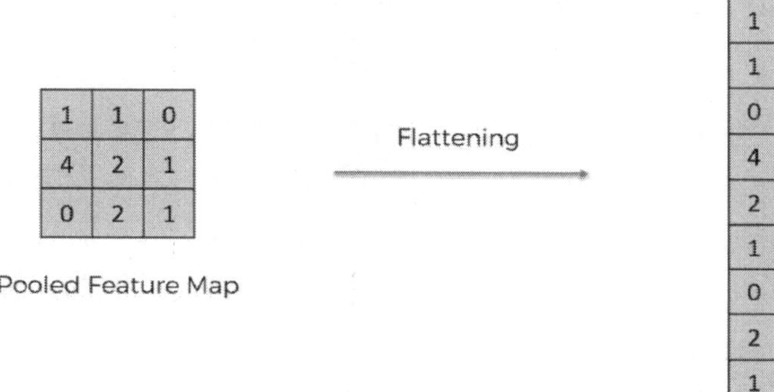

The one-dimensional vector is then used as input to the densely or fully connected neural network layer that you saw in project 3. This is shown in the following image:

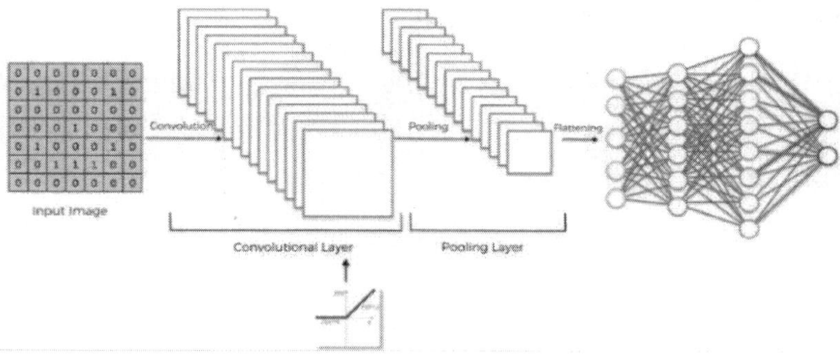

6.2. Cats and Dogs Image Classification with a CNN

In this section, we will move forward with the implementation of the convolutional neural network in Python. We know that a convolutional neural network can learn to identify the related features on a 2D map, such as images. In this project, we will solve the image classification task with CNN. Given a set of images, the task is to predict whether an image contains a cat or a dog.

Importing the Dataset and Required Libraries

The dataset for this project consists of images of cats and dogs. The dataset can be downloaded directly from this Kaggle Link (https://www.kaggle.com/c/dogs-vs-cats).

The dataset is also available inside the Animal Datasets, which is located inside the Datasets folder in the GitHub and SharePoint repositories. The original dataset consists of 2,500 images. But the dataset that we are going to use will be smaller and will consist of 10,000 images. Out of 10,000 images, 8,000 images are used for training, while 2,000 images are used for testing. The training set consists of 4,000 images of cats and 4,000 images of dogs. The test set also contains an equal number of images of cats and dogs.

It is important to mention that the dataset should be arranged in the following directory structure for TensorFlow Keras to extract images and their corresponding labels:

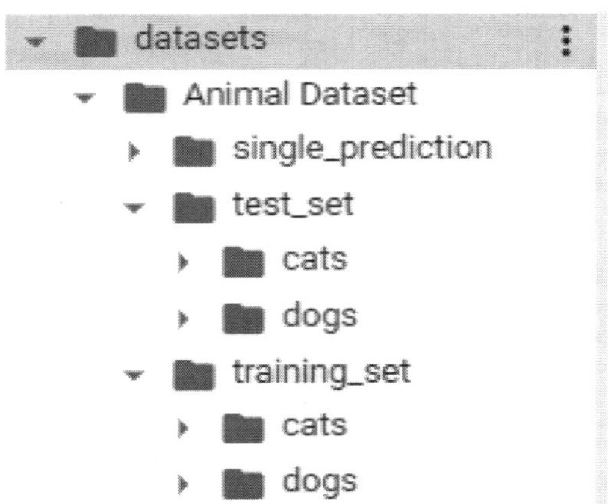

As a first step, upgrade to the latest version of the TensorFlow library.

Script 1:

```
pip install --upgrade tensorflow
```

The image dataset in this project is uploaded to Google Drive so that it can be accessed easily by the Google collaborator environment. The following script will mount your Google Drive in your Google Collaborator environment.

Script 2:

```
# mounting google drive
from google.colab import drive
drive.mount('/gdrive')
```

Let's import the TensorFlow Keras libraries necessary to create a convolutional neural network.

Script 3:

```
from tensorflow.keras.models import Sequential
from tensorflow.keras.layers import Conv2D
from tensorflow.keras.layers import MaxPooling2D
from tensorflow.keras.layers import Flatten
from tensorflow.keras.layers import Dense
```

6.2.1. Creating Model Architecture

In the previous two projects, we used the Keras Functional API to create the TensorFlow Keras model. The Functional API is good when you have to develop complex deep learning models. For simpler deep learning models, you can use Sequential API, as well. In this project, we will build our CNN model using sequential API.

To create a sequential model, you have to first create an object of the `Sequential` class from the `tensorflow.keras.models` module.

Script 4:

```
cnn_model = Sequential()
```

Next, you can create layers and add them to the Sequential model object that you just created.

The following script adds a convolution layer with 32 filters of shape 3 x 3 to the sequential model. Notice that the input shape size here is 64, 64, 3. This is because we will resize our images to a pixel size of 64 x 64 before training. The dimension 3 is added because a color image has three channels, i.e., red, green, and blue (RGB).

Script 5:

```
conv_layer1 = Conv2D (32, (3, 3), input_shape = (64, 64, 3), activation = 'relu')
cnn_model.add(conv_layer1)
```

Next, we will create a pooling layer of size 2, 2, and add it to our sequential CNN model, as shown below.

Script 6:

```
pool_layer1 = MaxPooling2D(pool_size = (2, 2))
cnn_model.add(pool_layer1)
```

Let's add one more convolution and one more pooling layer to our sequential model. Look at scripts 7 and 8 for reference.

Script 7:

```
conv_layer2 = Conv2D (32, (3, 3), input_shape = (64, 64, 3), activation = 'relu')
cnn_model.add(conv_layer2)
```

Script 8:

```
pool_layer2 = MaxPooling2D(pool_size = (2, 2))
cnn_model.add(pool_layer2)
```

You can add more convolutional and sequential layers if you want.

As you studied in the theory section, the convolutional and pooling layers are followed by dense layers. To connect the output of convolutional and pooling layers to dense layers, you need to flatten the output first using the `Flatten` layer, as shown below.

Script 9:

```
flatten_layer = Flatten()
cnn_model.add(flatten_layer )
```

We add two dense layers to our model. The first layer will have 128 neurons, and the second dense layer, which will also be the output layer, will consist of 1 neuron since we are predicting a single value. Scripts 10 and 11, shown below, add the final two dense layers to our model.

Script 10:

```
dense_layer1 = Dense(units = 128, activation = 'relu')
cnn_model.add(dense_layer1)
```

Script 11:

```
dense_layer2 = Dense(units = 1, activation = 'sigmoid')
cnn_model.add(dense_layer2)
```

As we did in the previous project, before training a model, we need to compile it. To do so, you can use the compile model, as shown below. The optimizer we used is `adam,` whereas the loss function is `binary_cross` entropy since we have only two possible outputs, i.e., whether an image can be a cat or a dog.

And since this is a classification problem, the performance metric has been set to `accuracy`.

Script 12:

```
cnn_model.compile(optimizer = 'adam', loss = 'binary_
crossentropy', metrics = ['accuracy'])
```

Let's plot our model to see its overall architecture:

Script 13:

```
#plotting model architecture
from tensorflow.keras.utils import plot_model
plot_model(cnn_model, to_file='/gdrive/My Drive/datasets/
model_plot1.png', show_shapes=True, show_layer_names=True)
```

Output:

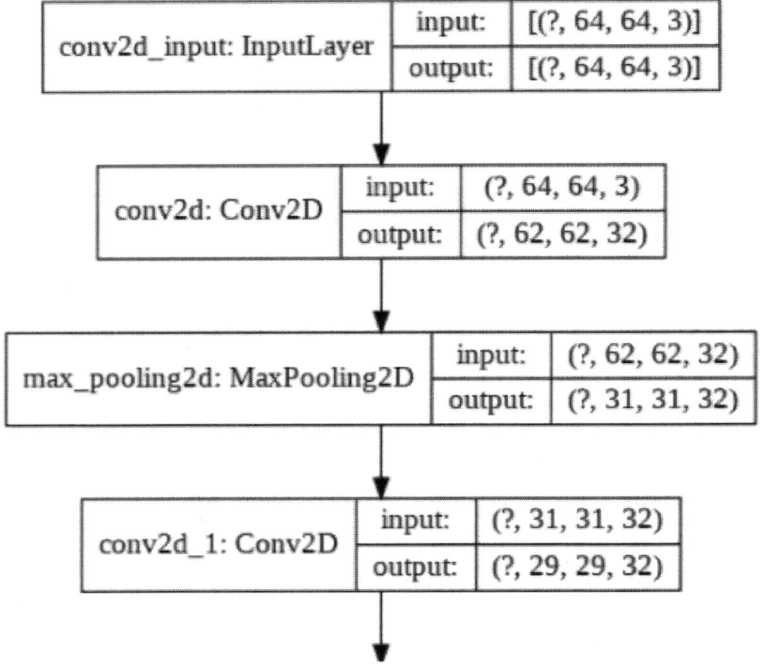

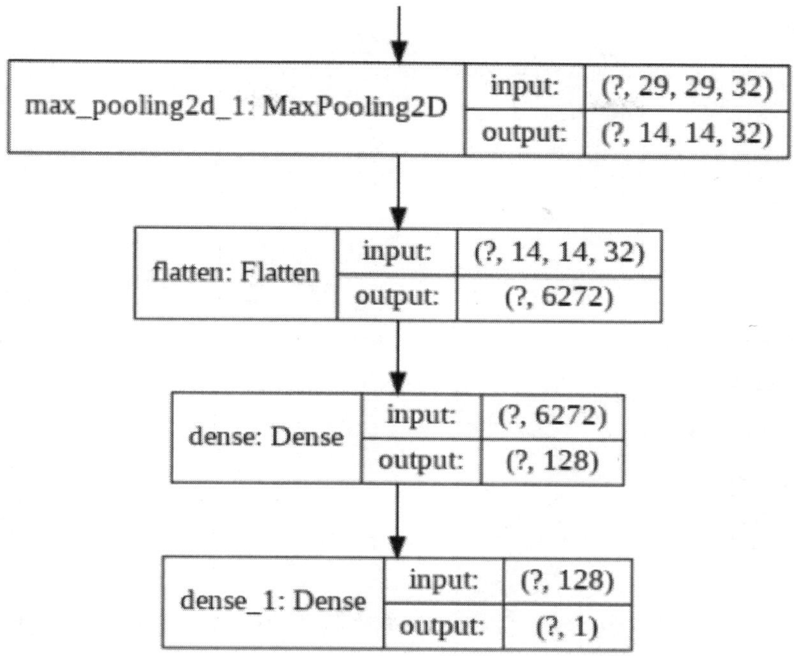

6.2.2. Image Augmentation

To improve the image and to increase the image uniformity, you can apply several preprocessing steps to an image. To do so, you can use the `ImageDataGenerator` class from the `tensorflow.keras.preprocessing.image module`. The following script applies feature scaling to the training and test images by dividing each pixel value by 255. Next, a shear value and zoom range of 0.2 is also added to the image. Finally, all the images are flipped horizontally.

To know more about `ImageDataGenerator` class, take a look at this official documentation link: https://keras.io/api/preprocessing/image/.

The following script applies image augmentation to the training set.

Script 14:

```
from tensorflow.keras.preprocessing.image import ImageDataGenerator

train_generator  = ImageDataGenerator(rescale = 1./255,
                                      shear_range = 0.2,
                                      zoom_range = 0.2,
                                      horizontal_flip = True)
```

And the following script applies image augmentation to the test set. Note that we only apply feature scaling to the test set, and no other preprocessing step is applied to the test set.

Script 15:

```
test_generator = ImageDataGenerator(rescale = 1./255)
```

6.2.3. Dividing Data into Training & Test Sets

Next, we need to divide the data into training and test sets. Since the images are in a local directory, you can use the `flow_from_directory()` method of the `ImageDataGenerator` object for the training and test sets.

You need to specify the target size (image size), which is 64, 64 in our case. The batch size defines the number of images that will be processed in a batch. And finally, since we have two output classes for our dataset, the `class_mode` attribute is set to binary.

The following script creates the final training and test sets.

Script 16:

```
training_data = train_generator.flow_from_directory(r'/gdrive/My Drive/datasets/Animal Dataset/training_set',
                                                    target_size = (64, 64),
                                                    batch_size = 32,
                                                    class_mode = 'binary')

test_data = test_generator.flow_from_directory('/gdrive/My Drive/datasets/Animal Dataset/test_set',
                                                    target_size = (64, 64),
                                                    batch_size = 32,
                                                    class_mode = 'binary')
```

6.2.4. Training a CNN Model

Training the model is easy. You just need to pass the training and test sets to the fit() method of your CNN model. You need to specify the steps per epoch. Steps per epoch refers to the number of times you want to update the weights of your neural network in one epoch. Since we have 8,000 records in the training set where 32 images are processed in a bath, the steps per epoch will be 8000/32 = 250. Similarly, in the test set, we process 32 images at a time. The validation step is also set to 2000/32, which means that the model will be validated on the test set after a batch of 32 images.

Script 17:

```
cnn_model.fit(training_data,
                        steps_per_epoch = (8000/32),
                        epochs = 25,
                        validation_data = test_data,
                        validation_steps = (2000/32))
```

The output after 25 epochs is as follows. An accuracy of 88.49 percent is achieved on the training set, while an accuracy of 75.80 is achieved on the test set.

Output:

```
250/250 [==============================] - 92s 369ms/step - loss: 0.3285 - accuracy: 0.8558 - val_loss: 0.4478 - val_accuracy: 0.8000
Epoch 20/25
250/250 [==============================] - 93s 372ms/step - loss: 0.3259 - accuracy: 0.8558 - val_loss: 0.4693 - val_accuracy: 0.8010
Epoch 21/25
250/250 [==============================] - 96s 386ms/step - loss: 0.3094 - accuracy: 0.8633 - val_loss: 0.5065 - val_accuracy: 0.7815
Epoch 22/25
250/250 [==============================] - 93s 373ms/step - loss: 0.2957 - accuracy: 0.8736 - val_loss: 0.4739 - val_accuracy: 0.8015
Epoch 23/25
250/250 [==============================] - 93s 371ms/step - loss: 0.2866 - accuracy: 0.8759 - val_loss: 0.4887 - val_accuracy: 0.7930
Epoch 24/25
250/250 [==============================] - 89s 356ms/step - loss: 0.2738 - accuracy: 0.8841 - val_loss: 0.4953 - val_accuracy: 0.8060
Epoch 25/25
250/250 [==============================] - 89s 357ms/step - loss: 0.2712 - accuracy: 0.8849 - val_loss: 0.6055 - val_accuracy: 0.7580
<tensorflow.python.keras.callbacks.History at 0x7f79b94356a0>
```

6.2.5. Making Prediction on a Single Image

Let's now see how you can make predictions on a single image. If you look at the single_prediction folder in your dataset, it contains two images: cat_or_dog_1.jpg and cat_or_dog2.jpg. We will be predicting what is in the first image, i.e., cat_or_dog1.jpg.

Execute the following script to load the cat_or_dog1.jpg image and convert it into an image of 64 x 64 pixels.

Script 18:

```
import numpy as np
from tensorflow.keras.preprocessing import image

single_image = image.load_img("/gdrive/My Drive/datasets/Animal Dataset/single_prediction/cat_or_dog_1.jpg", target_size= (64, 64))
```

Let's look at the image type.

Script 19:

```
type(single_image)
```

Output:

```
PIL.Image.Image
```

The image type is PIL. We need to convert it into array type so that our trained CNN model can make predictions on it. To do so, you can use the `img_to_array()` function of the image from the `tensorflow.keras.preprocessing` module, as shown below.

Script 20:

```
single_image = image.img_to_array(single_image)
single_image = np.expand_dims(single_image, axis = 0)
```

The above script also adds one extra dimension to the image array because the trained model is trained using an extra dimension, i.e., batch. Therefore, while making a prediction, you also need to add the dimension for the batch. Though the batch size for a single image will always be 1, you still need to add the dimension in order to make a prediction.

Finally, to make predictions, you need to pass the array for the image to the `predict()` method of the CNN model, as shown below:

Script 21:

```
image_result = cnn_model.predict(single_image)
```

The prediction made by a CNN model for binary classification will be 0 or 1. To check the index values for 0 and 1, you can use the following script.

Script 22:

```
training_data.class_indices
```

The following output shows that 0 corresponds to a cat while 1 corresponds to a dog.

Output:

```
{'cats': 0, 'dogs': 1}
```

Let's print the value of the predicted result. To print the value, you need to first specify the batch number and image number. Since you have only one batch and only one image within that batch, you can specify 0 and 0 for both.

Script 23:

```
1. print(image_result[0][0])
```

Output:

```
1.0
```

The output depicts a value of 1.0, which shows that the predicted image contains a dog. To verify, open the image Animal Dataset/single_prediction/cat_or_dog_1.jpg, and you should see that it actually contains an image of a dog, as shown below. This means our prediction is correct!

Further Readings – Image Classification with CNN

To study more about image classification with TensorFlow Keras, take a look at these links:
https://bit.ly/3ed8PCg
https://bit.ly/2TFijwU

Exercise 6.1

Question 1

What should be the input shape of the input image to the convolutional neural network?

A. Width, Height

B. Height, Width

C. Channels, Width, Height

D. Width, Height, Channels

Question 2

The pooling layer is used to pick correct features even if:

A. Image is inverted

B. Image is distorted

C. Image is compressed

D. All of the above

Question 3

The ReLu activation function is used to introduce:

A. Linearity

B. Non-linearity

C. Quadraticity

D. None of the above

PROJECT

7

Movie Recommender System Using Item-Based Collaborative Filtering

Recommender systems, also labeled recommendation systems, are statistical algorithms that recommend products to users based on similarities between the buying trends of various users or similarities between the products.

In this project, you will see how to create a simple movie recommendation system, which recommends movies to a user using item-based collaborative filtering. Before you see the actual code for the recommendation system, let's first understand what collaborative filtering is.

7.1. What Is Collaborative Filtering?

The process used to calculate similarities between the buying trends of various users or similarities between products is called collaborative filtering. Collaborative filtering can be, on the whole, classified into two types: User-based collaborative filtering and item-based collaborative filtering.

User-Based Collaborative Filtering

User-based collaborative filtering is dependent on user choices. For example, in a recommender system based on user-based collaborative filtering, if two users, X and Y, like products A and B and there is another user Z who likes product A, the product B will be recommended to user Z.

One of the main disadvantages of user-based collaborative filtering is that user choices evolve over time. In addition, the number of users is higher than products. Hence, creating user-based collaborative filtering becomes a complex task statistically.

Item-Based Collaborative Filtering

In item-based collaborative filtering, products are recommended based on similarities between themselves. For instance, if a user likes product A and product A has properties X and Y, another product B with properties X and Y will also be recommended to the user.

Item-based collaborative filtering is eliminating user dependency, and even if user choices change over time, the properties of products remain unchanged. Hence, recommendation systems based on collaborative filtering are not time-dependent.

In the next section, you will implement a recommender system based on item-based collaborative filtering that recommends movies to users based on the similarities between the movie ratings. So, let's begin without much ado.

7.2. Importing the Required Libraries

The first step, as always, is to install the required libraries. Execute the following script for that.

Script 1:

```
import numpy as np
import pandas as pd
import matplotlib.pyplot as plt
import seaborn as sns
```

7.3. Importing the Dataset

You import the dataset next. The dataset for this project can be downloaded free from this link (https://grouplens.org/datasets/movielens/latest/). From the link, download the compressed folder named "ml-latest-small.zip." If you extract the folder, you should see various CSV files. From these files, you will only need *movies.csv* and *ratings.csv*. The files are also available inside the folder *ml-latest-small* found in the *Datasets* directory in the GitHub and SharePoint repositories.

The dataset contains around 100,000 movie reviews applied to 9,000 movies by 600 users.

Let's first import the movies.csv file. The file script uses the `read_csv()` method from the Pandas library to read the CSV file into a Pandas dataframe. Next, the `head()` method of the Pandas dataframe is being used to display the header of the dataset.

Script 2:

```
movie_ids_titles = pd.read_csv(r"E:/Datasets/ml-latest-small/movies.csv")
movie_ids_titles.head()
```

Output:

	movieId	title	genres
0	1	Toy Story (1995)	Adventure|Animation|Children|Comedy|Fantasy
1	2	Jumanji (1995)	Adventure|Children|Fantasy
2	3	Grumpier Old Men (1995)	Comedy|Romance
3	4	Waiting to Exhale (1995)	Comedy|Drama|Romance
4	5	Father of the Bride Part II (1995)	Comedy

From the above output, you can see that the *movies.csv* file contains three columns, i.e., movieId, title, and genres. This dataframe basically maps the movieId with the movie title.

Next, import the ratings.csv file using the following script.

Script 3:

```
1. movie_ids_ratings = pd.read_csv(r"E:/Datasets/ml-latest-
   small/ratings.csv")
2. movie_ids_ratings.head()
```

Output:

	userId	movieId	rating	timestamp
0	1	1	4.0	964982703
1	1	3	4.0	964981247
2	1	6	4.0	964982224
3	1	47	5.0	964983815
4	1	50	5.0	964982931

The *ratings.csv* file contains the userId column, which contains the ID of the user who rated a movie. The movieId column consists of the id of the movie; the rating column consists of ratings, while the timestamp column consists of the timestamp (in seconds) when the review was left.

Let's see the shape of the `movie_ids_ratings` dataframe.

Script 4:

```
1. movie_ids_ratings.shape
```

Output:

```
(100836, 4)
```

The output shows that we have 100,836 records, and each record has four columns.

7.4. Data Preprocessing

We need a dataframe that consists of userId, movieId, title, and ratings. We can create such a dataframe by merging `movie_ids_titles` and `movie_ids_ratings` dataframe using the movieId column since the movieId column is the same between the two dataframes. However, before that, we will remove the genres column from the `movie_ids_titles` dataframe and the timestamp column from the `movie_ids_ratings` dataframe. The following script removes the genres column from the `movie_ids_titles` dataframe.

Script 5:

```
1. movie_ids_titles.drop("genres", inplace = True, axis = 1)
2. movie_ids_titles.head()
```

Output:

	movieId	title
0	1	Toy Story (1995)
1	2	Jumanji (1995)
2	3	Grumpier Old Men (1995)
3	4	Waiting to Exhale (1995)
4	5	Father of the Bride Part II (1995)

Similarly, the following script removes the timestamp column from the `movie_ids_ratings` dataframe.

Script 6:

```
movie_ids_ratings.drop("timestamp", inplace = True, axis = 1)
movie_ids_ratings.head()
```

Output:

	userId	movieId	rating
0	1	1	4.0
1	1	3	4.0
2	1	6	4.0
3	1	47	5.0
4	1	50	5.0

Now, we can merge the `movie_ids_titles` and `movie_ids_ratings` dataframe to create our desired dataframe. Execute the following script to merge the two dataframes on the common column, i.e., `movieId`.

Script 7:

```
merged_movie_df = pd.merge(movie_ids_ratings, movie_ids_titles, on='movieId')
merged_movie_df.head()
```

Output:

	userId	movieId	rating	title
0	1	1	4.0	Toy Story (1995)
1	5	1	4.0	Toy Story (1995)
2	7	1	4.5	Toy Story (1995)
3	15	1	2.5	Toy Story (1995)
4	17	1	4.5	Toy Story (1995)

7.5. Data Visualization

Data visualization is an important step and can reveal important information about the data.

Let's first group the dataset by title and see what information we can get regarding the ratings of movies. Execute the following script.

Script 8:

```
1. merged_movie_df.groupby('title').describe()
```

Output:

	userId								movieId					rating				
	count	mean	std	min	25%	50%	75%	max	count	mean	...	75%	max	count	mean	std	min	25%
title																		
'71 (2014)	1.0	610.000000	NaN	610.0	610.00	610.0	610.00	610.0	1.0	117867.0	...	117867.0	117867.0	1.0	4.000000	NaN	4.0	4.000
'Hellboy': The Seeds of Creation (2004)	1.0	332.000000	NaN	332.0	332.00	332.0	332.00	332.0	1.0	97757.0	...	97757.0	97757.0	1.0	4.000000	NaN	4.0	4.000
'Round Midnight (1986)	2.0	354.500000	31.819805	332.0	343.25	354.5	365.75	377.0	2.0	26564.0	...	26564.0	26564.0	2.0	3.500000	0.000000	3.5	3.500
'Salem's Lot (2004)	1.0	345.000000	NaN	345.0	345.00	345.0	345.00	345.0	1.0	27751.0	...	27751.0	27751.0	1.0	5.000000	NaN	5.0	5.000
'Til There Was You (1997)	2.0	229.000000	164.048773	113.0	171.00	229.0	287.00	345.0	2.0	779.0	...	779.0	779.0	2.0	4.000000	1.414214	3.0	3.500
...	...	...	...	...	...	...	...	...	...	...	...	...	...	...	...	...	...	...
eXistenZ (1999)	22.0	389.954545	167.161022	95.0	278.25	419.5	509.25	608.0	22.0	2600.0	...	2600.0	2600.0	22.0	3.863636	0.804479	2.0	3.500
xXx (2002)	24.0	272.916667	174.297576	9.0	131.25	240.5	418.50	610.0	24.0	5507.0	...	5507.0	5507.0	24.0	2.770833	0.966607	0.5	2.375
xXx: State of the Union (2005)	5.0	386.000000	148.801882	232.0	274.00	382.0	432.00	610.0	5.0	33158.0	...	33158.0	33158.0	5.0	2.000000	0.500000	1.5	1.500
¡Three Amigos! (1986)	26.0	279.807692	193.794947	1.0	101.25	260.5	441.25	599.0	26.0	2478.0	...	2478.0	2478.0	26.0	3.134615	0.944009	1.0	2.500
À nous la liberté (Freedom for Us) (1931)	1.0	527.000000	NaN	527.0	527.00	527.0	527.00	527.0	1.0	5560.0	...	5560.0	5560.0	1.0	1.000000	NaN	1.0	1.000

9719 rows × 24 columns

The output above shows the userId, movieId, and rating columns grouped together with respect to the title column. The `describe()` method further shows the information as mean, min, max, and standard deviation values for userId, movieId, and rating columns. We are only interested in the ratings column. To extract the mean of ratings grouped by title, you can use the following script.

Script 9:

```
1. merged_movie_df.groupby('title')['rating'].mean().head()
```

The output below shows that the first two movies got an average rating of 4.0 each, while the third and fourth movies have average ratings of 3 and 5, respectively.

Output:

```
title
'71 (2014)                                   4.0
'Hellboy': The Seeds of Creation (2004)     4.0
'Round Midnight (1986)                       3.5
'Salem's Lot (2004)                          5.0
'Til There Was You (1997)                    4.0
Name: rating, dtype: float64
```

Let's sort the movie titles by the descending order of the average user ratings. Execute the following.

Script 10:

```
1. merged_movie_df.groupby('title')['rating'].mean().sort_
   values(ascending=False).head()
```

The output below shows the names of some not so famous movies. This is possible because some unknown movies might have got high ratings but only by a few users. Hence, we can say that average rating alone is not a good criterion to judge a movie. The number of times a movie has been rated is also important.

Output:

```
title
Karlson Returns (1970)                              5.0
Winter in Prostokvashino (1984)                     5.0
My Love (2006)                                      5.0
Sorority House Massacre II (1990)                   5.0
Winnie the Pooh and the Day of Concern (1972)       5.0
Name: rating, dtype: float64
```

Let's now print the movies in the descending order of their rating counts.

Script 11:

```
1. merged_movie_df.groupby('title')['rating'].count().sort_
   values(ascending=False).head()
```

Here is the output. You can now see some really famous movies, which shows that a movie that is rated by a large number of people is usually a good movie.

Output:

```
title
Forrest Gump (1994)                    329
Shawshank Redemption, The (1994)       317
Pulp Fiction (1994)                    307
Silence of the Lambs, The (1991)       279
Matrix, The (1999)                     278
Name: rating, dtype: int64
```

Let's create a new dataframe that shows the title, mean rating, and the rating counts. Execute the following two scripts.

Script 12:

```
1. movie_rating_mean_count = pd.DataFrame(columns=['rating_
   mean', 'rating_count'])
```

Script 13:

```
movie_rating_mean_count["rating_mean"] = merged_movie_df.groupby('title')['rating'].mean()
movie_rating_mean_count["rating_count"] = merged_movie_df.groupby('title')['rating'].count()

movie_rating_mean_count.head()
```

The following output shows the final dataframe. The dataframe now contains the movie title, average ratings (rating_mean), and the number of rating counts (rating_count).

Output:

title	rating_mean	rating_count
'71 (2014)	4.0	1
'Hellboy': The Seeds of Creation (2004)	4.0	1
'Round Midnight (1986)	3.5	2
'Salem's Lot (2004)	5.0	1
'Til There Was You (1997)	4.0	2

First, we will plot a histogram to see how the average ratings are distributed.

Script 14:

```
plt.figure(figsize=(10,8))
sns.set_style("darkgrid")
movie_rating_mean_count['rating_mean'].hist(bins=30, color = "purple")
```

The output below shows that most of the movies have an average rating between 3 and 4.

Output:

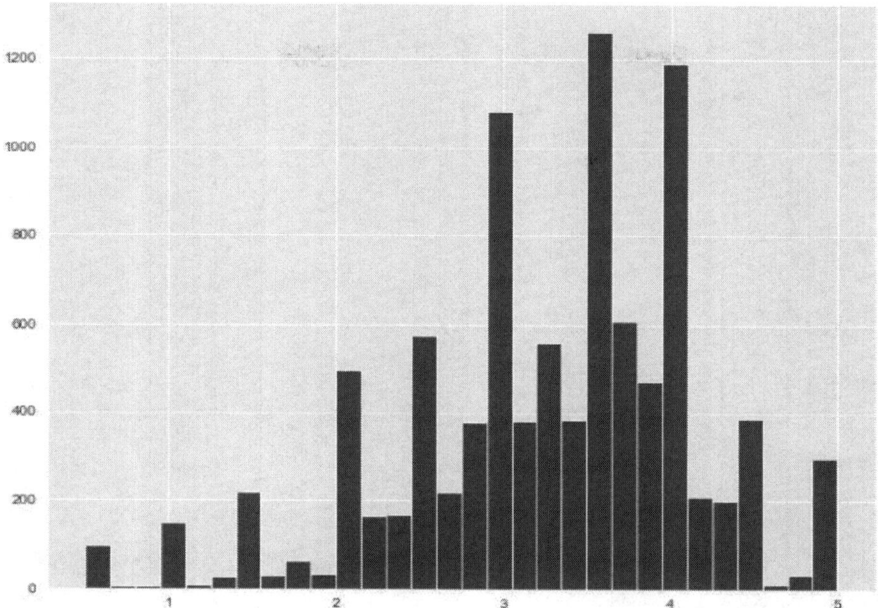

Next, let's plot the distribution of rating counts.

Script 15:

```
plt.figure(figsize=(10,8))
sns.set_style("darkgrid")
movie_rating_mean_count['rating_count'].hist(bins=33,
color = "green")
```

The output below shows that there are around 7,000 movies with less than 10 rating counts. The number of movies decreases with an increase in rating counts. Movies with more than 50 ratings are very few.

Output:

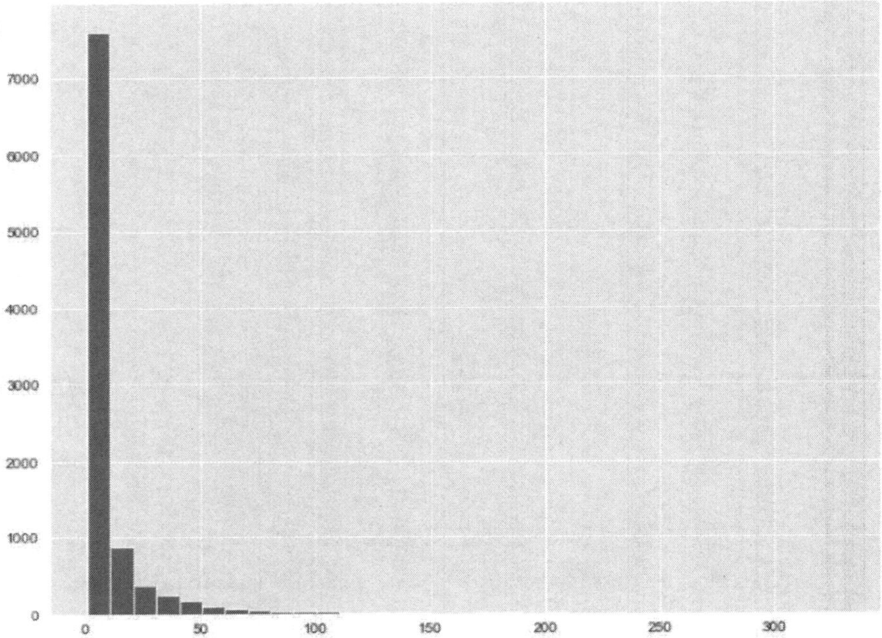

Finally, it is also interesting to see the relationship between the mean ratings and rating counts of a movie. You can plot a scatter plot for that, as shown in the following script:

Script 16:

```
plt.figure(figsize=(10,8))
sns.set_style("darkgrid")
sns.regplot(x="rating_mean", y="rating_count", data=movie_
rating_mean_count, color = "brown")
```

If you look at the top right portion of the following output, you can see that the movies with a higher number of rating counts tend to have higher mean ratings as well.

Output:

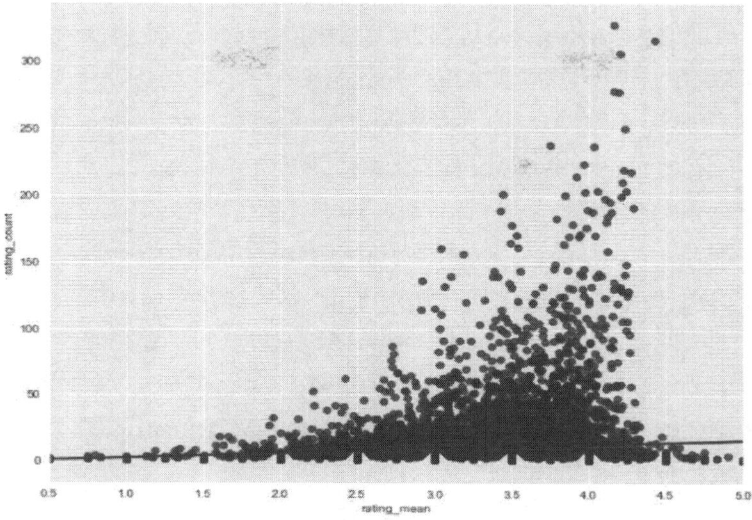

Let's sort our dataset by rating counts and see the average ratings of the movies with the top 5 highest number of ratings.

Script 17:

```
1. movie_rating_mean_count.sort_values("rating_count",
   ascending = False).head()
```

Again, you can see from the following output that movies with a higher number of ratings counts have average ratings of more than 5.

Output:

title	rating_mean	rating_count
Forrest Gump (1994)	4.164134	329
Shawshank Redemption, The (1994)	4.429022	317
Pulp Fiction (1994)	4.197068	307
Silence of the Lambs, The (1991)	4.161290	279
Matrix, The (1999)	4.192446	278

Enough of data visualization. The next step is to recommend movies based on collaborative filtering.

7.6. Item-based Collaborative Filtering

As discussed earlier, we will be creating a movie recommender system based on item-based collaborative filtering. In item-based collaborative filtering, products are recommended based on common characteristics. For instance, in a movie recommender system based on item-based collaborative filtering, a common characteristic for recommending movies could be the director of a movie, the actors in the movie, and so on and so forth. In our dataset, we have average ratings for different movies given by different users. We will use the average ratings as the common characteristic of the collaborative filtering of movies.

The first step is to create a dataframe where each movie is represented by a column and rows contain user ratings for movies. To create such a dataframe, you can use the `pivot_table()` function of a Pandas dataframe as follows.

Script 18:

```
user_movie_rating_matrix = merged_movie_df.pivot_
table(index='userId', columns='title', values='rating')
user_movie_rating_matrix
```

Look at the output below. Here, the user Ids represent the dataframe index, whereas columns represent movie titles. A single cell contains the rating left by a particular user for a particular movie. You can see many null values in the following dataframe because every user didn't rate every movie.

Output:

title userId	'71 (2014)	'Hellboy': The Seeds of Creation (2004)	'Round Midnight (1986)	'Salem's Lot (2004)	'Til There Was You (1997)	'Tis the Season for Love (2015)	'burbs, The (1989)	'night Mother (1986)	(500) Days of Summer (2009)	*batteries not included (1987)	...	Zulu (2013)	[REC] (2007)	[REC]² (2009)	[REC]³ 3 Génesis (2012)	anohana: The Flower We Saw That Day - The Movie (2013)	eXistenZ (1999)	x) (2
1	NaN	NaN	NaN	NaN	NaN	NaN	NaN	NaN	NaN	NaN	...	NaN	NaN	NaN	NaN	NaN	NaN	
2	NaN	NaN	NaN	NaN	NaN	NaN	NaN	NaN	NaN	NaN	...	NaN	NaN	NaN	NaN	NaN	NaN	
3	NaN	NaN	NaN	NaN	NaN	NaN	NaN	NaN	NaN	NaN	...	NaN	NaN	NaN	NaN	NaN	NaN	
4	NaN	NaN	NaN	NaN	NaN	NaN	NaN	NaN	NaN	NaN	...	NaN	NaN	NaN	NaN	NaN	NaN	
5	NaN	NaN	NaN	NaN	NaN	NaN	NaN	NaN	NaN	NaN	...	NaN	NaN	NaN	NaN	NaN	NaN	
...	...	...	...	...	...	...	...	...	...	...	...	...	...	...	...	...	...	
606	NaN	NaN	NaN	NaN	NaN	NaN	NaN	NaN	NaN	NaN	...	NaN	NaN	NaN	NaN	NaN	NaN	
607	NaN	NaN	NaN	NaN	NaN	NaN	NaN	NaN	NaN	NaN	...	NaN	NaN	NaN	NaN	NaN	NaN	
608	NaN	NaN	NaN	NaN	NaN	NaN	NaN	NaN	NaN	NaN	...	NaN	NaN	NaN	NaN	NaN	4.5	
609	NaN	NaN	NaN	NaN	NaN	NaN	NaN	NaN	NaN	NaN	...	NaN	NaN	NaN	NaN	NaN	NaN	
610	4.0	NaN	NaN	NaN	NaN	NaN	NaN	NaN	3.5	NaN	...	NaN	4.0	3.5	3.0	NaN	NaN	

610 rows × 9719 columns

Let's plot the shape of our new dataframe.

Script 19:

```
1. user_movie_rating_matrix.shape
```

The output shows that our dataset contains 610 rows and 9,719 columns. This is because our dataset contains 610 unique users and 9,719 unique movies.

Output:

```
(610, 9719)
```

Next, we will find movie recommendations based on a single movie and then based on multiple movies.

7.6.1. Finding Recommendations Based on a Single Movie

Suppose we want to find recommendations based on the movie *Pulp Fiction* (1994). First, we will filter the column that contains the user ratings for the movie. The following script does that.

Script 20:

```
pulp_fiction_ratings = user_movie_rating_matrix["Pulp Fiction (1994)"]
```

Next, we will find the correlation between the user ratings of all the movies and the user ratings for the movie *pulp fiction*. We know that the `user_movie_rating_matrix` that we created earlier contains user ratings of all the movies in columns. Therefore, we need to find the correlation between the dataframe that contains user ratings for *Pulp Fiction* (1994), which is `pulp_fiction_ratings`, and the dataframe that contains user ratings for all the movies, i.e., `user_movie_rating_matrix`. To do so, you can use the `corrwith()` function, as shown in the following script. The newly created `pf_corr` column will contain the correlation between the ratings for the movie *Pulp Fiction* (1994) and all the other movies.

Script 21:

```
pulp_fiction_correlations = pd.DataFrame(user_movie_rating_matrix.corrwith(pulp_fiction_ratings), columns =["pf_corr"])
```

Let's print the first five movies with the highest correlation with the movie *Pulp Fiction* (1994). Execute the following script.

Script 22:

```
pulp_fiction_correlations.sort_values("pf_corr", ascending=False).head(5)
```

Here is the output. The names of the movies in the output below are not very well known. This shows that correlation itself is not a very good criterion for item-based collaborative filtering. For example, there can be a movie in the dataset that is rated 5 stars by only one user who also rated the movie *Pulp Fiction* (1994) as 5 stars. In such a case, that movie will have the highest correlation with *Pulp Fiction* (1994) since both the movies will have 5-star ratings.

Output:

title	pf_corr
Rare Exports: A Christmas Tale (Rare Exports) (2010)	1.0
Azumi (2003)	1.0
Maxed Out: Hard Times, Easy Credit and the Era of Predatory Lenders (2006)	1.0
War Zone, The (1999)	1.0
Wolfman, The (2010)	1.0

One solution to this problem can be that in addition to the correlation between the movies, we also use rating counts for the correlated movie as a criterion for finding the best recommendation. The following script adds the rating count for each movie in the `pulp_fiction_correlations` dataframe.

Script 23:

```
1. pulp_fiction_correlations = pulp_fiction_correlations.
   join(movie_rating_mean_count["rating_count"])
```

Next, let's plot the first five rows of the `pulp_fiction_correlations` dataframe.

Script 24:

```
1. pulp_fiction_correlations.head()
```

From the output, you can see both the `pf_corr` and `rating_count` columns. The `pf_corr` column contains some NaN values. This is because there can be movies that are rated by users who did not rate *Pulp Fiction* (1994). In such cases, the correlation will be null.

Output:

title	pf_corr	rating_count
'71 (2014)	NaN	1
'Hellboy': The Seeds of Creation (2004)	NaN	1
'Round Midnight (1986)	NaN	2
'Salem's Lot (2004)	NaN	1
'Til There Was You (1997)	NaN	2

We will remove all the movies with null correlation with *Pulp Fiction* (1994). Execute the following script to do so.

Script 25:

```
1. pulp_fiction_correlations.dropna(inplace = True)
```

Next, plot the movies with the highest correlation with *Pulp Fiction* (1994).

Script 26:

```
1. pulp_fiction_correlations.sort_values("pf_corr",
   ascending=False).head(5)
```

You can see from the output below that, as expected, the movies with the highest correlation have very low rating counts, and, hence, the correlation doesn't give a true picture of the similarities between movies.

Output:

title	pf_corr	rating_count
Rare Exports: A Christmas Tale (Rare Exports) (2010)	1.0	2
Azumi (2003)	1.0	2
Maxed Out: Hard Times, Easy Credit and the Era of Predatory Lenders (2006)	1.0	2
War Zone, The (1999)	1.0	2
Wolfman, The (2010)	1.0	2

A better way is to find the movies with rating counts of at least 50 and having the highest correlation with *Pulp Fiction* (1994). The following script finds and prints those movies.

Script 27:

```
pulp_fiction_correlations_50 = pulp_fiction_correlations[pulp_fiction_correlations['rating_count']>50]
pulp_fiction_correlations_50.sort_values('pf_corr', ascending=False).head()
```

From the output below, you can see that the movie *Pulp Fiction* has the highest correlation with itself, which makes sense. Next, the highest correlation is found for the movies *The Wolf of Wall Street* (2013) and *Fight Club* (1999). These are the two movies recommended by our recommender system to a user who likes *Pulp Fiction* (1994).

Output:

title	pf_corr	rating_count
Pulp Fiction (1994)	1.000000	307
Wolf of Wall Street, The (2013)	0.579915	54
Fight Club (1999)	0.543465	218
Kill Bill: Vol. 1 (2003)	0.504147	131
Interstellar (2014)	0.503411	73

7.6.2. Finding Recommendations Based on Multiple Movies

In this section, you will see how to recommend movies to a user based on his ratings of multiple movies. The first step is to create a dataframe, which contains a correlation between all the movies in our dataset in the form of a matrix. To do so, you can use the `corr()` method of the Pandas dataframe. The correlation type, which is Pearson, in this case, is passed to the method parameter. The `min_periods` attribute value specifies the minimum number of observations required per pair of columns to have a valid result. A `min_periods` value of 50 specifies calculating correlation for only those pair of movies that have been rated by at least 50 same users. For the rest of the movie pairs, the correlation will be null.

Script 28:

```
all_movie_correlations = user_movie_rating_matrix.
corr(method = 'pearson', min_periods = 50)
```

Let's plot the header of the `all_movie_correlations` dataframe.

Script 29:

```
all_movie_correlations.head()
```

Output:

title	'71 (2014)	'Hellboy': The Seeds of Creation (2004)	'Round Midnight (1986)	'Salem's Lot (2004)	'Til There Was You (1997)	'Tis the Season for Love (2015)	'burbs, The (1989)	'night Mother (1986)	(500) Days of Summer (2009)	*batteries not included (1987)	...	Zulu (2013)	[REC] (2007)	[REC]² (2009)	[REC]³ 3 Génesis (2012)	anohana: The Flower We Saw That Day - The Movie (2013)	eXistenZ (1999)
title																	
'71 (2014)	NaN	NaN	NaN	NaN	NaN	NaN	NaN	NaN	NaN	NaN	...	NaN	NaN	NaN	NaN	NaN	NaN
'Hellboy': The Seeds of Creation (2004)	NaN	NaN	NaN	NaN	NaN	NaN	NaN	NaN	NaN	NaN	...	NaN	NaN	NaN	NaN	NaN	NaN
'Round Midnight (1986)	NaN	NaN	NaN	NaN	NaN	NaN	NaN	NaN	NaN	NaN	...	NaN	NaN	NaN	NaN	NaN	NaN
'Salem's Lot (2004)	NaN	NaN	NaN	NaN	NaN	NaN	NaN	NaN	NaN	NaN	...	NaN	NaN	NaN	NaN	NaN	NaN
'Til There Was You (1997)	NaN	NaN	NaN	NaN	NaN	NaN	NaN	NaN	NaN	NaN	...	NaN	NaN	NaN	NaN	NaN	NaN

5 rows × 9719 columns

Now suppose a new user logs into your website. The user has already watched three movies and has given a rating to those movies. Let's create a new dataframe that contains fictional ratings given by a user to three movies.

Script 30:

```
movie_data = [['Forrest Gump (1994)', 4.0], ['Fight Club (1999)', 3.5], ['Interstellar (2014)', 4.0]]


test_movies = pd.DataFrame(movie_data, columns = ['Movie_Name', 'Movie_Rating'])
test_movies.head()
```

Our input dataframe looks like this. We will be recommending movies from our dataset based on the ratings given by a new user for these three movies.

Output:

	Movie_Name	Movie_Rating
0	Forrest Gump (1994)	4.0
1	Fight Club (1999)	3.5
2	Interstellar (2014)	4.0

To get the name and ratings of a movie from the `test_movie` dataframe, you can use the following script.

Script 31:

```
print(test_movies['Movie_Name'][0])
print(test_movies['Movie_Rating'][0])
```

Output:

```
Forrest Gump (1994)
4.0
```

From the `all_movie_correlations` dataframe, let's obtain correlation values for the movies related to *Forrest Gump* (1994). The movies with null correlation are dropped. Execute the following script.

Script 32:

```
all_movie_correlations['Forrest Gump (1994)'].dropna()
```

Output:

```
title
2001: A Space Odyssey (1968)                        0.191558
300 (2007)                                          0.321523
40-Year-Old Virgin, The (2005)                      0.156517
Ace Ventura: Pet Detective (1994)                   0.137870
Ace Ventura: When Nature Calls (1995)               0.421868
                                                       ...
Willy Wonka & the Chocolate Factory (1971)          0.195081
Wizard of Oz, The (1939)                            0.162368
X-Men (2000)                                        0.200786
X2: X-Men United (2003)                             0.246717
Young Frankenstein (1974)                           0.230049
Name: Forrest Gump (1994), Length: 313, dtype: float64
```

Now, you know how to obtain names and ratings of movies from the `test_movie` dataframe and how to obtain correlations of all the movies with a single movie using the movie title.

Next, we will iterate through the three movies in the `test_movie` dataframe, find the correlated movies, and then multiply the correlation of all the correlated movies with the ratings of the input movie. The correlated movies, along with the weighted correlation (calculated by multiplying the actual correlation with the ratings of the movies in the `test_movie` dataframe), are appended to an empty series named `recommended_movies`.

Script 33:

```
recommended_movies = pd.Series()
for i in range(0, 2):
    movie = all_movie_correlations[test_movies['Movie_Name'][i]].dropna()
    movie  = movie.map(lambda movie_corr: movie_corr * test_movies['Movie_Rating'][i])
    recommended_movies = recommended_movies.append(movie)
```

The newly created list of recommended_movies looks like this:

Script 34:

```
recommended_movies
```

Output:

```
2001: A Space Odyssey (1968)                        0.766231
300 (2007)                                          1.286094
40-Year-Old Virgin, The (2005)                      0.626066
Ace Ventura: Pet Detective (1994)                   0.551479
Ace Ventura: When Nature Calls (1995)               1.687472
                                                      ...
Who Framed Roger Rabbit? (1988)                     0.874334
Willy Wonka & the Chocolate Factory (1971)          0.663971
Wizard of Oz, The (1939)                           -0.971160
X-Men (2000)                                       -0.063318
X2: X-Men United (2003)                            -0.661265
Length: 529, dtype: float64
```

To get a final recommendation, you can sort the movies in the descending order of the weighted correlation, as shown below.

Script 35:

```
recommended_movies.sort_values(inplace = True, ascending =
False)
print (recommended_movies.head(10))
```

The output shows the list of recommended movies based on the movies *Forrest Gump* (1994), *Fight Club* (1999), and *Interstellar* (2014).

Output:

```
Forrest Gump (1994)                                   4.000000
Fight Club (1999)                                     3.500000
Mr. Holland's Opus (1995)                             2.608575
Lock, Stock & Two Smoking Barrels (1998)              2.570366
Django Unchained (2012)                               2.225161
Life Is Beautiful (La Vita è bella) (1997)            2.203741
Pocahontas (1995)                                     2.200471
Big (1988)                                            1.969404
Good Will Hunting (1997)                              1.936169
Pulp Fiction (1994)                                   1.902128
dtype: float64
```

You can see from the above output that *Forrest Gump* (1994) and *Fight Club* (1999) have the highest correlation with themselves. Hence, they are recommended. The movie *Interstellar* (2014) doesn't appear on the list because it might not have passed the minimum 50 ratings thresholds. The remaining movies are the movies recommended by our recommender system to a user who watched *Forrest Gump* (1994), *Fight Club* (1999), and *Interstellar* (2014).

Further Readings – Recommender Systems

To study more about recommender systems, check out these links:
https://bit.ly/38trc5j
https://bit.ly/2GEmmXa

Exercise 7.1

Question 1:

What is the disadvantage of user-based collaborative filtering?

A. Users taste changes over time

B. More users than items

C. Complex and a higher number of computations

D. All of the above

Question 2:

Which method is used to find the correlation between columns of two different Pandas dataframes?

A. get_corr()

B. corr()

C. corrwith()

D. None of the above()

Question 3:

Which method is used to find the correlation between the columns of a single dataframe?

A. get_corr()

B. corr()

C. corrwith()

D. corrself()

PROJECT

Face Detection with OpenCV in Python

Face detection, as the name suggests, refers to detecting faces from images or videos and is one of the commonest computer vision tasks. Face detection is a precursor to many advanced tasks such as emotion detection, interest detection, surprise detection, etc. Face detection is also the first step in developing face recognition systems.

Various algorithms have been developed for face recognition tasks. However, for this project, we will use the Viola-Jones Algorithm (https://bit.ly/3mVUZYe) for object detection. It is a very simple algorithm and can detect objects such as faces in images with very high accuracy.

8.1. OpenCV for Face Detection

OpenCV (https://opencv.org/) stands for Open Computer Vision Library and is one of the oldest yet, frequently used computer vision library. OpenCV was initially developed in C++. However, you will be using the Python wrapper for OpenCV in this project. The good thing about the Python wrapper for OpenCV is that it comes with trained instances of the Viola-Jones algorithm for detecting face, lip, smile, body, etc., and you do not have to implement the Viola-Jones algorithm yourself.

To install OpenCV for Python, execute the following script on your command terminal:

```
pip install opencv-python
```

Next, you will see how you can detect the faces, eyes, and smiles of humans using the Viola-Jones algorithm implemented in OpenCV wrapper for Python. So, let's begin without much ado.

8.2. Installing the Libraries and Importing Images

Let's import the required libraries first.

Script 1:

```
# pip install opencv-python
import cv2

import matplotlib.pyplot as plt
%matplotlib inline
```

For detecting face, eyes, and lips, we will be using two images. One image contains a single person, and the other image contains multiple persons. Both the images are available in the *face_images* folder inside the *Datasets* directory in the GitHub and SharePoint repositories.

Let's import both the images first. To do so, you can use the `imread()` function of the OpenCV library and pass it the image path.

Script 2:

```
1. image1 = cv2.imread(r"E:/Datasets/face_images/image1.jpg", 0)
2. image2 = cv2.imread(r"E:/Datasets/face_images/image2.jpg", 0)
```

The following script displays *image1* in grayscale form.

Script 3:

```
plt.imshow(image1, cmap ="gray")
```

Output:

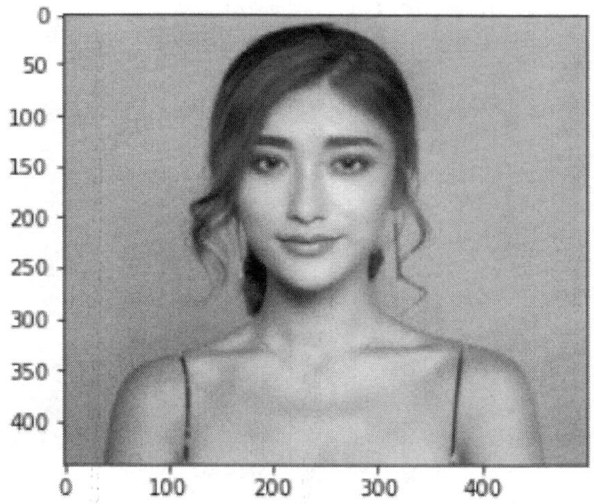

Let's now try to detect the face in the above image.

8.3. Detecting Whole Faces

As I said earlier, you will be using the Viola-Jones algorithm for object detection in order to detect face, eyes, and lips. The trained algorithms are installed with OpenCV. To access the XML files containing the algorithm, you need to pass the path of the algorithm to the `CascadeClassifier()` method of OpenCV. To find the path of XML files containing the algorithm, execute the following script.

Script 4:

```
cv2.data.haarcascades
```

In the output, you will see a path to the haarcascade files for the Viola-Jones algorithm.

Output:

```
C:\ProgramData\Anaconda3\Lib\site-packages\cv2\data
```

If you go to the path that contains your haarcascade files, you should see the following files and directories:

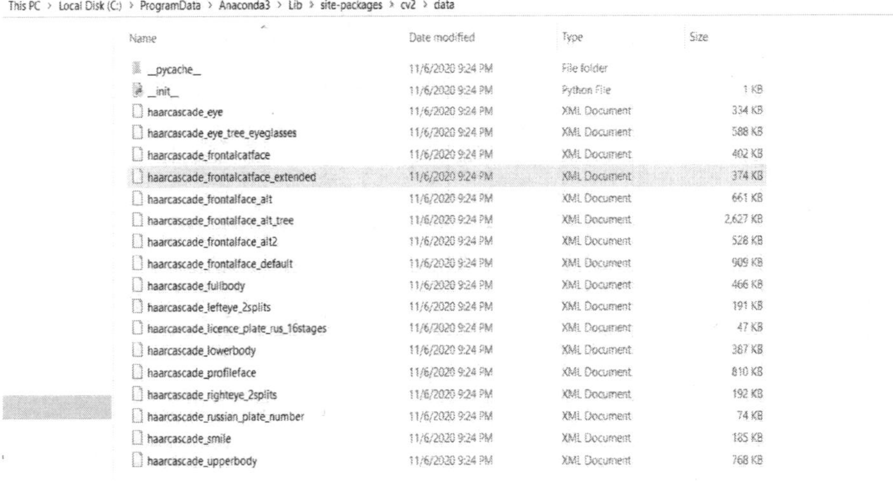

For face detection, initially, you will be using the "haarcascade_frontalface_default.xml" file. To import the corresponding algorithm contained by the file, execute the following script.

Script 5:

```
face_detector = cv2.CascadeClassifier(cv2.data.haarcascades +
'haarcascade_frontalface_default.xml')
```

Next, you need to define a method, which accepts an image. To detect a face inside that image, you need to call the `detectMultiscale()` method of the face detector object that you initialized in Script 5. Once the face is detected, you need to create a rectangle around the face. To do so, you need the x and y components of the face area and the width and height of the face. Using that information, you can create a rectangle by calling the rectangle method of the OpenCV object. Finally, the image with a rectangle around the detected face is returned by the function. The **detect_face()** method in the following script performs these tasks.

Script 6:

```
def detect_face (image):

    face_image = image.copy()

    face_rectangle = face_detector.detectMultiScale(face_image)

    for (x,y,width,height) in face_rectangle:
        cv2.rectangle(face_image, (x,y), (x + width, y+height), (255,255,255), 8)

    return face_image
```

To detect the face, simply pass the face object to the **detect_face()** method that you defined in Script 6. The following script passes image1 to the **detect_face()** method.

Script 7:

```
detection_result = detect_face(image1)
```

Finally, to plot the image with face detection, pass the image returned by the **detect_face()** method to the **imshow()** method of the OpenCV module, as shown below.

Script 8:

```
plt.imshow(detection_result, cmap = "gray")
```

In the following output, you can see that the face has been detected successfully in the image.

Output:

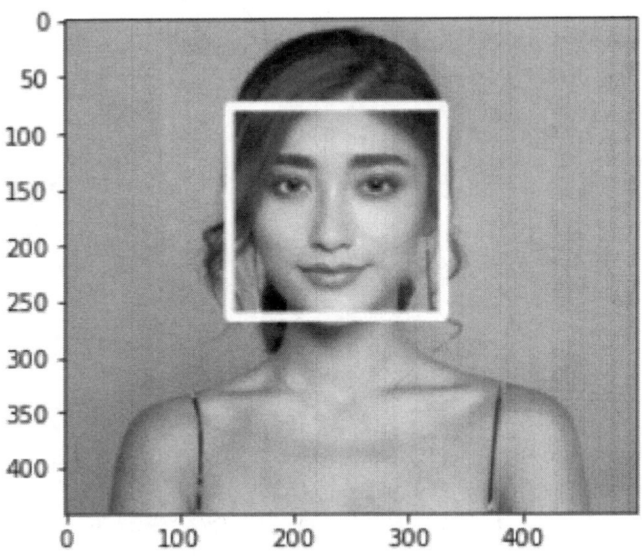

Let's now try to detect faces from *image2*, which contains faces of nine persons. Execute the following script:

Script 9:

```
detection_result = detect_face(image2)
plt.imshow(detection_result, cmap = "gray")
```

The output below shows that out of nine persons in the image, the faces of six persons are detected successfully.

Output:

OpenCV contains other classifiers as well for face detection. For instance, in the following script, we define a `detect_face()` method, which uses the "haarcascade_frontalface_alt.xml" classifier for face detection. The following script tries to detect faces in *image2*.

Script 10:

```
face_detector = cv2.CascadeClassifier(cv2.data.haarcascades + 'haarcascade_frontalface_alt.xml')

def detect_face (image):

    face_image = image.copy()

    face_rectangle = face_detector.detectMultiScale(face_image)

    for (x,y,width,height) in face_rectangle:
        cv2.rectangle(face_image, (x,y), (x + width, y+height), (255,255,255), 8)

```

```
    return face_image

detection_result = detect_face(image2)
plt.imshow(detection_result, cmap = "gray")
```

The output below shows that now 7 out of 9 images are detected which means that "haarcascade_frontalface_alt" classifier performed better than "haarcascade_frontalface_default" classifier.

Output:

Finally, let's use another face detection classifier i.e. "haarcascade_frontalface_tree" to see how many faces can it detect in "image2".

Script 11:

```
face_detector = cv2.CascadeClassifier(cv2.data.haarcascades + 'haarcascade_frontalface_alt_tree.xml')

def detect_face (image):

    face_image = image.copy()

    face_rectangle = face_detector.detectMultiScale(face_image)

    for (x,y,width,height) in face_rectangle:
        cv2.rectangle(face_image, (x,y), (x + width, y+height), (255,255,255), 8)

    return face_image

detection_result = detect_face(image2)
plt.imshow(detection_result, cmap = "gray")
```

The output shows that "haarcascade_frontalface_tree" only detects three faces with default settings.

Output:

8.4. Detecting Eyes

In addition to detecting faces, you can detect eyes in a face as well. To do so, you need the *haarcascade_eye* classifier. The following script creates an object of *haarcascade_eye* classifier.

Script 12:

```
eye_detector = cv2.CascadeClassifier(cv2.data.haarcascades + 'haarcascade_eye.xml')
```

And the following script defines the detect_eye() method, which detects eyes from a face and then plots rectangles around eyes.

Script 13:

```
def detect_eye (image):

    face_image = image.copy()

    face_rectangle = eye_detector.detectMultiScale(face_image)

    for (x,y,width,height) in face_rectangle:
        cv2.rectangle(face_image, (x,y), (x + width, y+height), (255,255,255), 8)

    return face_image
```

Finally, the following script passes *image1* to the detect_eye() method.

Script 14:

```
detection_result = detect_eye(image1)
```

The image returned by the detect_eye()method is plotted via the following script.

Script 15:

```
plt.imshow(detection_result, cmap = "gray")
```

From the output below, you can see that the eyes have been successfully detected from the *image1*.

Output:

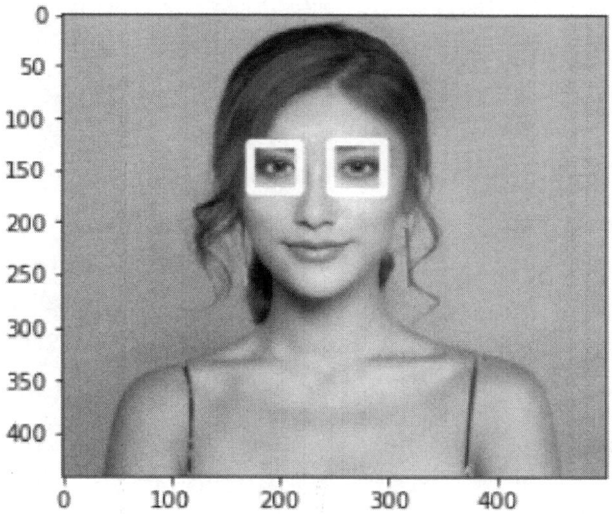

The following script tries to detect eyes inside the faces in *image2*.

Script 16:

```
detection_result = detect_eye(image2)
plt.imshow(detection_result, cmap = "gray")
```

The output below shows that in addition to detecting eyes, some other portions of the face have also been wrongly detected as eyes.

Output:

To avoid detecting extra objects in addition to the desired objects, you need to update the values of the `scaleFactor` and `minNeigbours` attributes of the `detectMultiScale()` method of various **haarcascade** classifier objects. For instance, to avoid detecting extra eyes in *image2*, you can update the `detectMultiScale()` method of the **eye_detector** object of the *haarcascade_eye* classifier, as follows. Here, we set the value of `scaleFactor` to 1.2 and the value of **minNeighbors** to 4.

Script 17:

```
def detect_eye (image):

    face_image = image.copy()

    face_rectangle = eye_detector.detectMultiScale(face_image, scaleFactor = 1.2, minNeighbors =4)

    for (x,y,width,height) in face_rectangle:
        cv2.rectangle(face_image, (x,y), (x + width, y+height), (255,255,255), 8)

    return face_image
```

Basically, the scaleFactor is used to create your scale pyramid. Your model has a fixed size specified during training, which is visible in the xml. Hence, if this size of the face is present in the image, it is detected. By rescaling the input image, however, a larger face can be resized to a smaller one, making it detectable by the algorithm.

The minNeighbors attribute specifies the number neighbors that each candidate rectangle should have in order to retain it. This parameter directly affects the quality of the detected faces. Higher values result in fewer detections but with higher quality.

There are no hard and fast rules for setting values for scaleFactor and minNeigbours attributes. You can play around with different values and select the ones that give you the best object detection results.

Let's now again try to detect eyes in *image2* using modified values of the scaleFactor and minNeigbours attributes.

Script 18:

```
detection_result = detect_eye(image2)
plt.imshow(detection_result, cmap = "gray")
```

The output shows that though there are still a few extra detections, however, the detections are still better than before.

Output:

8.5. Detecting Smile

You can also detect a smile within an image using OpenCV implementation of the Viola-Jones algorithm for smile detection. To do so, you can use the *haarcascade_smile* classifier, as shown in the following script.

Script 19:

```
1.  smile_detector = cv2.CascadeClassifier(cv2.data.
    haarcascades + 'haarcascade_smile.xml')
```

Next, we define a method `detect_smile()`, which detects smiles in the input image and draws rectangles around smiles.

Script 20:

```
def detect_smile (image):

    face_image = image.copy()

    face_rectangle = smile_detector .detectMultiScale(face_image)

    for (x,y,width,height) in face_rectangle:
        cv2.rectangle(face_image, (x,y), (x + width, y+height), (255,255,255), 8)

    return face_image
```

Finally, we pass *image1* for smile detection to the `detect_smile()` method.

Script 21:

```
detection_result = detect_smile(image1)
plt.imshow(detection_result, cmap = "gray")
```

The output below shows that we have plenty of extra detections. Hence, we need to adjust the values of the `scaleFactor` and `minNeigbours` attributes.

Output:

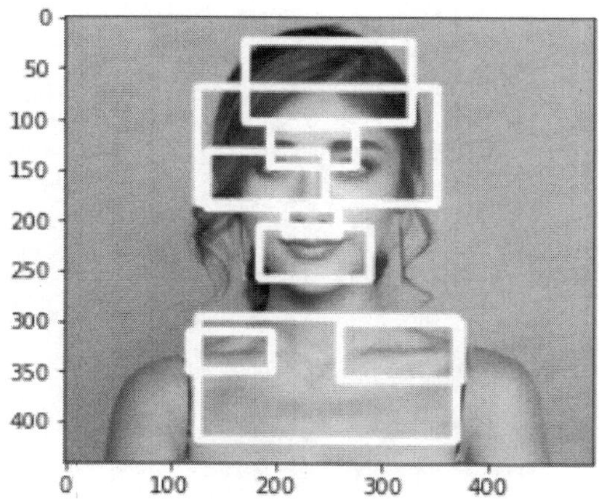

Modify the `detect_smile()` method as follows:

Script 22:

```python
def detect_smile (image):

    face_image = image.copy()

    face_rectangle = smile_detector.detectMultiScale(face_
image, scaleFactor = 2.0, minNeighbors =20)

    for (x,y,width,height) in face_rectangle:
        cv2.rectangle(face_image, (x,y), (x + width,
y+height), (255,255,255), 8)

    return face_image
```

Now, try to detect the smile in *image1* using the following script:

Script 23:

```python
detection_result = detect_smile(image1)
plt.imshow(detection_result, cmap = "gray")
```

You will get this output. You can see that all the extra detections have now been removed, and only the lips are detected for a smile.

Output:

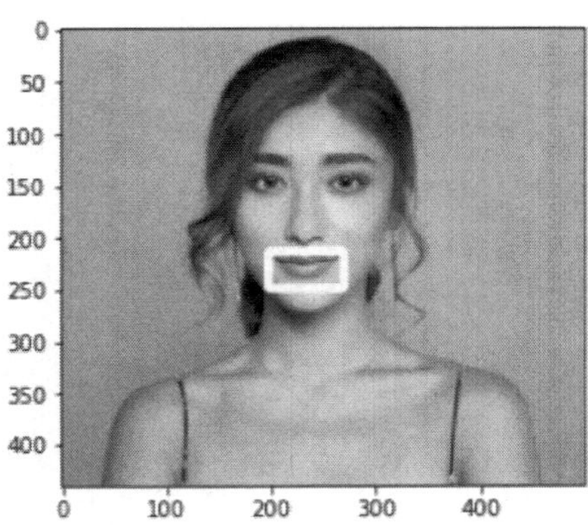

Finally, let's try to detect the lips in *image2*. Execute the following script:

Script 24:

```
detection_result = detect_smile(image2)
plt.imshow(detection_result, cmap = "gray")
```

The output shows that the lips of most of the people are detected.

Output:

8.6. Face Detection from Live Videos

Since videos are essentially multiple frames of images, you can use the Viola-Jones Classifier to detect faces in videos. Let's first define the `detect_face()` method, which uses the `"haarcascade_frontalface_default"` face detection classifier to detect faces and draw a rectangle around the face.

Script 25:

```
face_detector = cv2.CascadeClassifier(cv2.data.haarcascades + 'haarcascade_frontalface_default.xml')

def detect_face (image):

    face_image = image.copy()

    face_rectangle = face_detector.detectMultiScale(face_image)

    for (x,y,width,height) in face_rectangle:
        cv2.rectangle(face_image, (x,y), (x + width, y+height), (255,255,255), 8)

    return face_image
```

Next, to capture a video from your system camera, you can use the VideoCapture object of OpenCV and pass it 0 as a parameter. Next, to read the current frame, pass 0 as a parameter to the read() method of the VideoCapture object. The detected frame is passed to the detect_face() method, and the detected face bounded by a rectangle is displayed in the output. This process continues until you press the key "q."

Script 26:

```
live_cam = cv2.VideoCapture(0)

while True:
    ret, current_frame = live_cam.read(0)

    current_frame = detect_face(current_frame)

    cv2.imshow("Face detected", current_frame)

    key = cv2.waitKey(50)
    if key == ord("q"):
```

```
        break

live_cam.release()
cv2.destroyAllWindows()
```

Here is the screenshot of the output for detecting faces from videos.

Output:

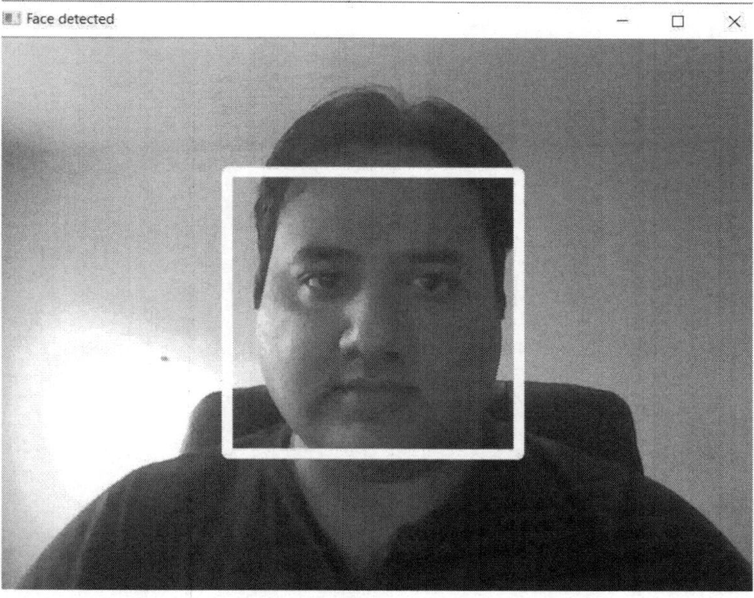

Further Readings – Open CV for Face Detection

To study more about face detection with OpenCV, check out these links:
https://opencv.org/
https://bit.ly/2IgitZo

Exercise 8.1

Question 1:

To decrease the number of detections, the value of the minNeighbours attribute of OpenCV Cascade Classifiers should be:

A. Increased

B. Decreased

C. Kept constant

D. All of the Above

Question 2:

Which of the following is not a cascade classifier for face detection in Open CV?

A. haarcascade_frontalface_alt_tree.xml

B. haarcascade_frontalface_alt.xml

C. haarcascade_frontalface_default_tree.xml

D. haarcascade_frontalface_default.xml

Question 3:

To capture a live video from the camera, which of the following values should be passed as an argument to the cv2. VideoCapture() method?

A. 0

B. 1

C. 2

D. 3

PROJECT

Handwritten English Character Recognition with CNN

Recognizing handwritten digits and characters is one of the most common tasks for the digitization of text. Digitization of handwritten text can be used to perform many natural language processing tasks such as text summarization, sentimental analysis, topic modeling, etc. The most basic task in handwritten text recognition is recognizing text characters. In this project, you will see how to recognize handwritten English text characters using Convolutional Neural Networks (CNN). You have already seen the application of CNN for cats and dogs image classification in project 6. In this article, you will be using a CNN for handwritten English alphabets. So, let's begin without much ado.

9.1. Importing the Required Libraries

The first step is to import the required libraries. You will be using the TensorFlow Keras library for CNN implementation. The following script imports the required libraries.

Script 1:

```
import numpy as np
import matplotlib.pyplot as plt

from tensorflow.keras.layers import Input,Conv2D, Dense, Flatten, Dropout, MaxPool2D

from tensorflow.keras.models import Model
```

9.2. Importing the Dataset

You will be using the EMNIST (Extended MNIST) dataset for this project. The EMNIST dataset contains various corpora containing images of handwritten digits and English alphabets. The details of the dataset are available at this link (https://bit.ly/38KhOKl).

The easiest way to download the EMNIST dataset is by installing Python's mnist module. To do so, execute the following PIP command on your terminal.

```
pip install mnist
```

Next, import the EMNIST module into your Python application by executing the following script.

Script 2:

```
from emnist import list_datasets
```

Let's see the list of available datasets in EMNIST. Run the following command.

Script 3:

```
list_datasets()
```

The EMNIST dataset has the following sub-datasets. The details of these datasets are available on the official link of the EMNIST website.

Output:

```
['balanced', 'byclass', 'bymerge', 'digits', 'letters',
'mnist']
```

We will be using the *letters* dataset, which contains a training set of 124,800 images and a test set of 20,800 images of 26 English alphabets. The following script imports the training images and labels.

Script 4:

```
from emnist import extract_training_samples
training_images, training_labels = extract_training_samples('letters')
```

And the following script imports the test images and labels.

Script 5:

```
from emnist import extract_test_samples
test_images, test_labels = extract_test_samples('letters')
```

Let's perform some data analysis and preprocessing before we train our CNN model for English alphabet recognition.

9.3. Data Analysis and Preprocessing

Let's first plot the shape of the training and test sets.

Script 6:

```
print(training_images.shape)
print(test_images.shape)
```

The output below shows that the training set contains 124,800 images of 28 x 28 pixels. Similarly, the test set contains 20,800 pixels of 28 x 28.

Output:

```
(124800, 28, 28)
(20800, 28, 28)
```

In the same way, you can plot the shape of the training and test labels.

Script 7:

```
print(training_labels.shape)
print(test_labels.shape)
```

Output:

```
(124800,)
(20800,)
```

Let's randomly plot the image number 3000 from the test set.

Script 8:

```
plt.figure()
plt.imshow(test_images[3000])
plt.colorbar()
plt.grid(False)
plt.show()
```

The output shows that the image at the 3,000th index of the test set contains the English letter D.

Output:

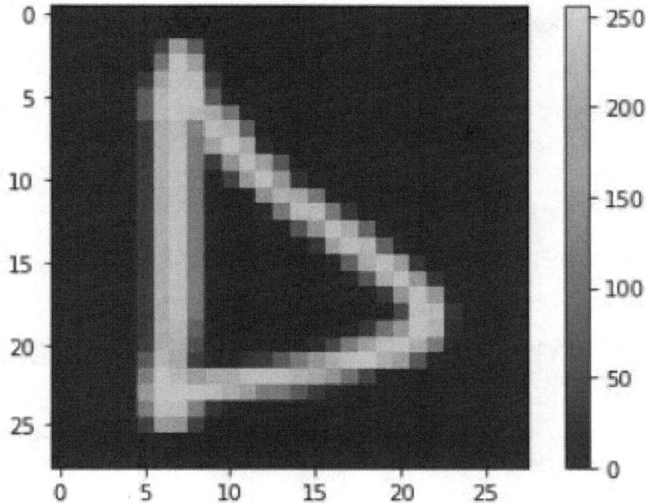

Let's plot the label for the image and see what we get.

Script 9:

```
print(test_labels[3000])
```

Output:

```
4
```

The label for the image D is 4. This is because the output labels contain integers for alphabets starting from 1 to 26. For instance, the label for image A is 1, and the label for image Z is 26. Since the letter D is the 4th alphabet in English ABC, the output label for the image at index 3,000 is 4.

Let's plot all the unique labels for images.

Script 10:

```
np.unique(test_labels)
```

Output:

```
array([ 1,  2,  3,  4,  5,  6,  7,  8,  9, 10, 11, 12, 13, 14,
15, 16, 17, 18, 19, 20, 21, 22, 23, 24, 25, 26], dtype=uint8)
```

The output shows that there are 26 unique labels, from 1 to 26.

The next step is to change the dimensions of our input images. CNN in Keras expect data to be in the format Width-Height-Channels. Our images contain width and height but no channels. Since the images are greyscale, we set the image channel to 1, as shown in the following script:

Script 11:

```
training_images = np.expand_dims(training_images, -1)
test_images = np.expand_dims(test_images, -1)
print(training_images.shape)
```

Output:

```
(124800, 28, 28, 1)
```

Let's store the number of unique labels in a variable *output_classes*. You will need this variable to specify the number of output classes in your neural network.

Script 12:

```
output_classes = len(set(training_labels))
```

9.4. Training and Fitting CNN Model

We are now ready to create our CNN model. In project 6, you used the Keras sequential API for developing a CNN model. Though you can use the sequential API for this project as well, you will be training your CNN model using the functional API. Functional API is much more flexible and powerful than sequential API.

In sequential API, you define the model first and then use the `add()` function to add layers to the model. In the case of functional API, you do not need the `add()` method.

With Keras functional API, to connect the previous layer with the next layer, the name of the previous layer is passed inside the parenthesis at the end of the next layer. You first define all the layers in a sequence and then simply pass the input and output layers to your CNN model.

The following script defines our CNN layers.

Script 13:

```
input_layer = Input(shape = training_images[0].shape )

conv1 = Conv2D(32, (3,3), strides = 2, activation= 'relu')
(input_layer)

maxpool1 = MaxPool2D(2, 2)(conv1)

conv2 = Conv2D(64, (3,3), strides = 2, activation= 'relu')
(maxpool1)

flat1 = Flatten()(conv2)

drop1 = Dropout(0.2)(flat1)

dense1 = Dense(512, activation = 'relu')(drop1)

drop2  = Dropout(0.2)(dense1)

output_layer = Dense(output_classes+1, activation=
'softmax')(drop2)
```

The CNN model defined in the above script contains one input layer, two convolutional layers, one flattening layer, one hidden dense layer, and one output layer. The number of filters in the first convolutional layer is 32, while the number of filters in the second convolutional layer is 64. The kernel size for both convolutional layers is 3 x 3, with a stride of 2. After the first convolutional layer, a max-pooling layer with a size 2 x 2 and stride 2 has also been defined. Dropout layers are also added after the flattening layer and the first dense layer. TensorFlow dropout layer is used to reduce overfitting. Overfitting occurs when the model performs better on the training set but worse on the test set.

The following script creates our CNN model. You can see that the input and output layers are passed as parameters to the mode.

Script 14:

```
model = Model(input_layer, output_layer)
```

The rest of the process is similar to what you did in project 6. Once the model is defined, you have to compile it, as shown below:

Script 15:

```
model.compile(optimizer = 'adam', loss= 'sparse_
   categorical_crossentropy', metrics =['accuracy'])
```

Finally, to train the model, you can use the `fit()` method, as shown below.

Script 16:

```
model_history = model.fit(training_images, training_labels,
   batch_size = 32, epochs=20, validation_data=(test_images,
   test_labels), verbose=1)
```

In the script above, the `batch_size` attribute specifies the number of records processed together for training, and **epochs** define the number of times the model is trained on the whole dataset. The `validation_data` attribute is used to specify the test set for evaluation. After 20 epochs, an accuracy of 87.06 is obtained on the test set.

Output:

```
Epoch 15/20
3900/3900 [==============================] - 22s 6ms/step - loss: 0.4399 - accuracy: 0.8530 - val_loss: 0.4231 - val_accuracy:
0.8667
Epoch 16/20
3900/3900 [==============================] - 19s 5ms/step - loss: 0.4402 - accuracy: 0.8511 - val_loss: 0.4051 - val_accuracy:
0.8657
Epoch 17/20
3900/3900 [==============================] - 19s 5ms/step - loss: 0.4336 - accuracy: 0.8551 - val_loss: 0.4014 - val_accuracy:
0.8675
Epoch 18/20
3900/3900 [==============================] - 22s 6ms/step - loss: 0.4323 - accuracy: 0.8537 - val_loss: 0.4121 - val_accuracy:
0.8692
Epoch 19/20
3900/3900 [==============================] - 21s 5ms/step - loss: 0.4305 - accuracy: 0.8550 - val_loss: 0.3917 - val_accuracy:
0.8737
Epoch 20/20
3900/3900 [==============================] - 19s 5ms/step - loss: 0.4262 - accuracy: 0.8568 - val_loss: 0.3962 - val_accuracy:
0.8706
```

9.5. Model Evaluation

Once the model is trained, and predictions are made on the test set, you have to evaluate it. There are several ways to do so. You can plot a graph showing the train and test accuracies against the number of epochs.

Script 17:

```
import matplotlib.pyplot as plt

plt.plot(model_history.history['accuracy'], label =
'accuracy')
plt.plot(model_history.history['val_accuracy'], label =
'val_accuracy')
plt.legend(['train','test'], loc='lower left')
```

The output below shows that our model performance increased on both training and test sets till the 5th epoch, and after that, the model performance remained stable. Since the accuracy on the test set is better than the accuracy on the training set, our model is not overfitting.

Output:

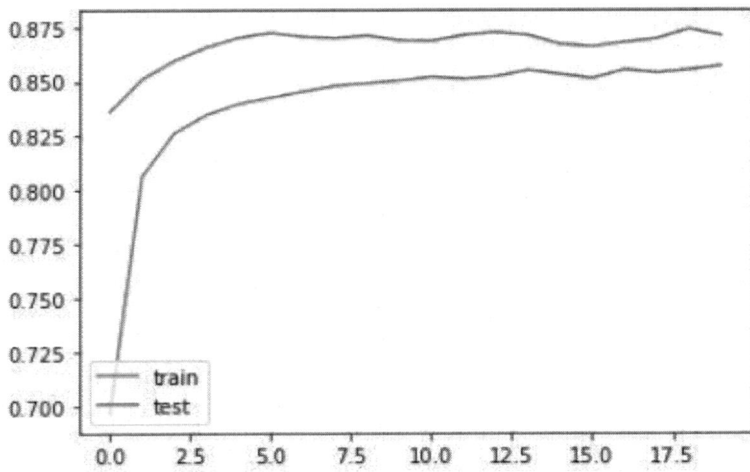

In addition to accuracy, you can also plot loss, as shown in the following script.

Script 18:

```
import matplotlib.pyplot as plt

plt.plot(model_history.history['loss'], label = 'loss')
plt.plot(model_history.history['val_loss'], label = 'val_loss')
plt.legend(['train','test'], loc='upper right')
```

The output below shows that the loss decreased till the 5th epoch, and the value of the testing loss is less than the training loss, which again shows that the model is not overfitting.

Output:

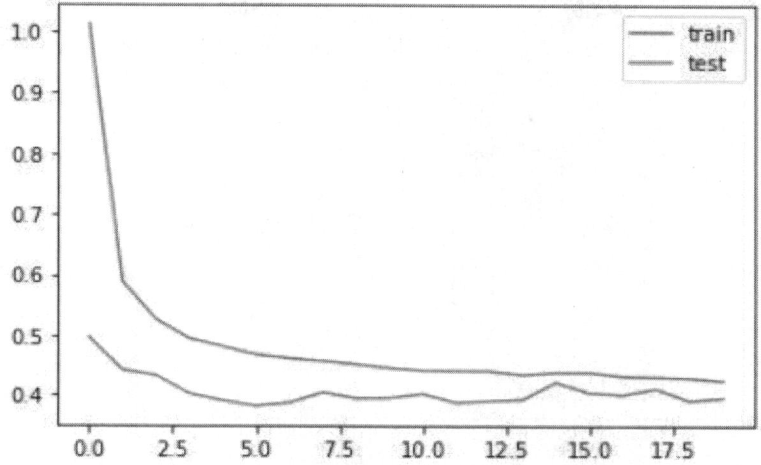

9.6. Making Predictions on a Single Image

Let's make a prediction on a single image. The following script imports the test set.

Script 19:

```
from emnist import extract_test_samples
test_images, test_labels = extract_test_samples('letters')
```

Let's select the image at the 2,000th index of the test set and plot it.

Script 20:

```
plt.figure()
plt.imshow(test_images[2000])
plt.colorbar()
plt.grid(False)
plt.show()
```

The output below shows that the image contains the digit C.

Output:

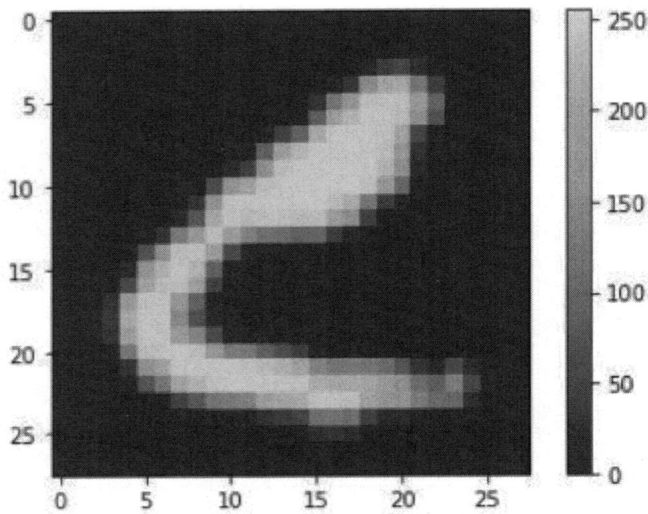

Let's plot the label for the image at index 2,000th of the test set.

Script 21:

```
print(test_labels[2000])
```

As expected, the label for image 2,000 contains digit 3.

Output:

```
3
```

In the next step, we will make a prediction on the 2000th image using our trained CNN and see what we get. The test set has to be passed to the `predict()` method to make a prediction on the test set, as shown below:

Script 22:

```
output = model.predict(test_images)
prediction = np.argmax(output[2000])
print(prediction)
```

Output:

```
3
```

Our model predicted 3 as the label for the image at index 2,000 of the test set, which is a correct prediction.

It is important to mention that you may get a different prediction since neural network weights are randomly initialized. However, the overall performance on the test set should remain around 86–87 percent.

Further Readings – English Letter Recognition with CNN

To study more about English letter recognition with CNN using TensorFlow Keras, take a look at these links:
https://keras.io/examples/vision/mnist_convnet/
https://bit.ly/2TFijwU

Exercise 9.1

Question 1:

Dropout layer is added in a TensorFlow Keras neural network to:

A. Increase Accuracy
B. Reduce Overfitting
C. Reduce Loss
D. Increase Overfitting

Question 2:

In Keras Functional API, which of the following functions is used to add layers to a neural network model?

A. add()
B. append()
C. insert()
D. None of the above()

Question 3:

Which of the following functions can be used to add a new dimension to a numpy array?

A. add_dims()
B. append_dims()
C. expand_dims()
D. insert_dims()

PROJECT

10

Customer Segmentation Based on Income and Spending

Successful marketing campaigns are based on customer characteristics. In order to increase revenue and maximize the cost-to-profit ratio of marketing campaigns, customers that are likely to spend more are particularly targeted. Therefore, it is important to identify such customers who have high incomes and are likely to spend more. In this project, you will see how to segment customers based on their incomes and past spending habits. You will then identify customers that have high incomes and higher spending.

Customer segmentation can be tackled as a clustering task where customers with similar incomes and shopping trends can be clustered together. Therefore, you will be using a clustering algorithm for customer segmentation in this project.

Clustering algorithms are unsupervised algorithms where the training data is not labeled. Rather, the algorithms cluster or group the data sets based on common characteristics. There are two main techniques for clustering data: K-Means clustering and Hierarchical clustering. In this project, you will use K-Means clustering for customer segmentation. Before you implement the actual code, let's first briefly review what K-Means clustering is.

10.1. K-Means Clustering

K-Means clustering is one of the most frequently used algorithms for clustering unlabeled data. In K-Means clustering K refers to the number of clusters that you want your data to be grouped into. In K-Means clustering, the number of clusters has to be defined before K clustering can be applied to the data points.

Steps for K-Means Clustering

Following are the steps that are needed to be performed in order to perform K-Means clustering of data points.

1. Randomly assign centroid values for each cluster
2. Calculate the distance (Euclidean or Manhattan) between each data point and centroid values of all the clusters.
3. Assign the data point to the cluster of the centroid with the shorted distance.
4. Calculate and update centroid values based on the mean values of the coordinates of all the data points of the corresponding cluster.
5. Repeat steps 2-4 until new centroid values for all the clusters are different from the previous centroid values.

Why Use K-Means Clustering?

K-Means clustering is particularly useful when:

1. K-Means clustering is a simple to implement algorithm
2. Can be applied to large datasets
3. Scales well to unseen data points
4. Generalize well to clusters of various sizes and shapes.

Disadvantages of K-Means Clustering Algorithm

The following are some of the disadvantages of the K-Means clustering algorithm.

1. The value of K has to be chosen manually.
2. Convergence or training time depends on the initial value of K.
3. Clustering performance is affected greatly by outliers.

Enough of theory. Let's see how to use K-Means clustering for customer segmentation.

10.2. Importing the Required Libraries

The first step is importing the required libraries, as shown in the following script:

Script 1:

```
import numpy as np
import pandas as pd
from sklearn.datasets.samples_generator import make_blobs
from sklearn.cluster import KMeans
from matplotlib import pyplot as plt
import seaborn as sns
%matplotlib inline
```

10.3. Importing the Dataset

The CSV dataset file for this project is freely available at this link (https://bit.ly/3kxXvCl). The CSV file for the dataset *Mall_Customers.csv* can also be downloaded from the *Data* folder of the GitHub and SharePoint repositories.

The following script imports the dataset.

Script 2:

```
1. dataset = pd.read_csv('E:\Datasets\Mall_Customers.csv')
```

The following script prints the first five rows of the dataset.

Script 3:

```
1. dataset.head()
```

The below output shows that the dataset has five columns: CustomerID, Genre, Age, Annual Income (K$), and Spending Score (1–100). The spending score is the score assigned to customers based on their previous spending habits. Customers with higher spending in the past have higher scores.

Output:

	CustomerID	Genre	Age	Annual Income (k$)	Spending Score (1-100)
0	1	Male	19	15	39
1	2	Male	21	15	81
2	3	Female	20	16	6
3	4	Female	23	16	77
4	5	Female	31	17	40

Let's see the shape of the dataset.

Script 4:

```
1. dataset.shape
```

The output below shows that the dataset contains 200 records and 5 columns.

Output

```
(200, 5)
```

10.4. Data Analysis

Before we do actual customer segmentation, let's briefly analyze the dataset. Let's plot a histogram showing the annual income of the customers.

Script 5:

```
1. sns.distplot(dataset['Annual Income (k$)'], kde=False,
   bins = 50)
```

The output shows that most of the customers have incomes between 60 and 90K per year.

Output:

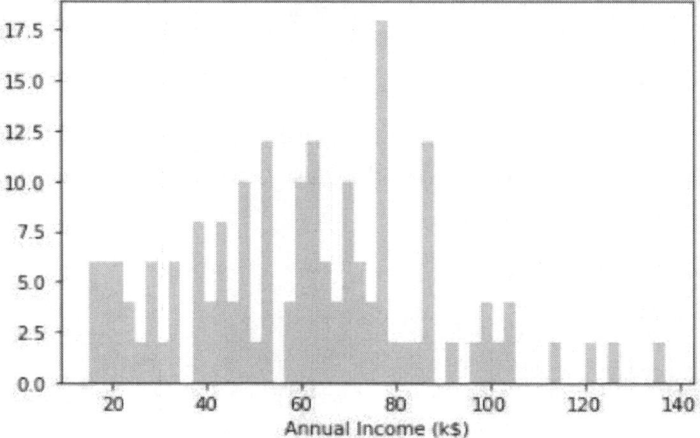

Similarly, we can plot a histogram for the spending scores of the customers, as well.

Script 6:

```
sns.distplot(dataset['Spending Score (1-100)'], kde=False,
bins = 50, color = "red")
```

The output shows that most of the customers have a spending score between 40 and 60.

Output:

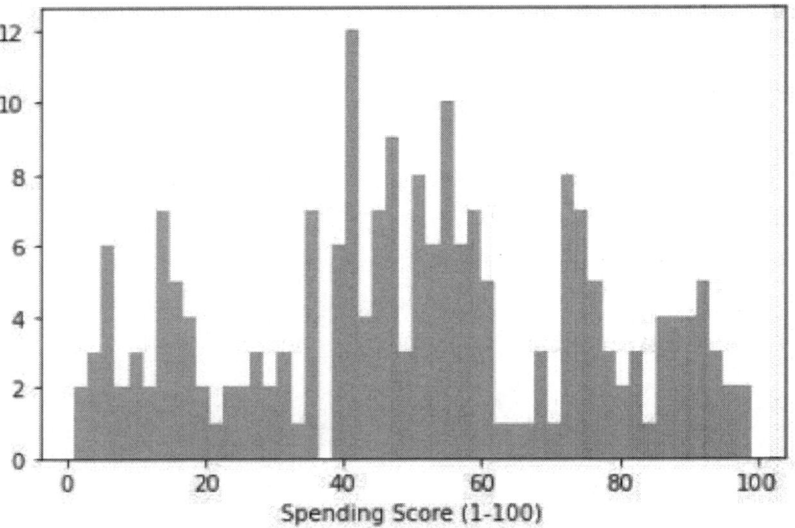

We can also plot a regression line between annual income and spending score to see if there is any linear relationship between the two or not.

Script 7:

```
sns.regplot(x="Annual Income (k$)", y="Spending Score (1-
100)", data=dataset)
```

From the straight line in the below output, you can infer that there is no linear relation between annual income and spending.

Output:

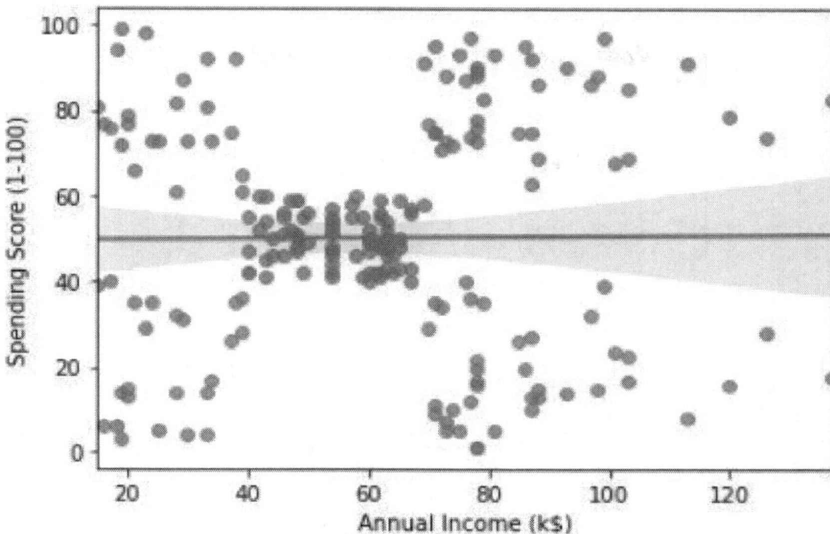

Finally, you can also plot a linear regression line between the Age column and the spending score.

Script 8:

```
sns.regplot(x="Age", y="Spending Score (1-100)", data=dataset)
```

The output confirms an inverse linear relationship between age and spending score. It can be inferred from the output that young people have higher spending compared to older people.

Output:

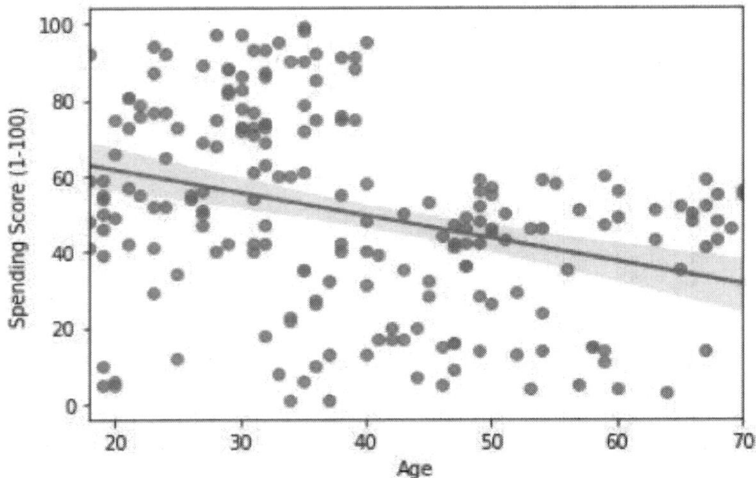

Enough of the data analysis. We are now ready to perform customer segmentation on our data using the K-Means algorithm.

10.5. K-Means Clustering

We want to perform K-Means clustering based on the annual income and spending score columns because we want to target the customer base with high income and high spending scores. Therefore, we will filter these two columns and will remove the remaining columns from our dataset. Here is the script to do so:

Script 9:

```
dataset = dataset.filter(["Annual Income (k$)", "Spending
Score (1-100)"], axis = 1)
dataset.head()
```

The output shows that we now have only the annual income and spending score columns in our dataset.

Output:

	Annual Income (k$)	Spending Score (1-100)
0	15	39
1	15	81
2	16	6
3	16	77
4	17	40

To implement K-Means clustering, you can use the `K-Means` class from the `sklearn.cluster` module of the `Sklearn library`. You have to pass the number of clusters as an attribute to the `K-Means` class constructor. To train the K-Means model, simply pass the dataset to the `fit()` method of the K-Means class, as shown below.

Script 10:

```
# performing kmeans clustering using KMeans class
km_model = KMeans(n_clusters=4)
km_model.fit(dataset)
```

Output

```
KMeans(n_clusters=4)
```

Once the model is trained, you can print the cluster centers using the `cluster_centers_` attribute of the `K-Means` class object.

Script 11:

```
#printing centroid values
print(km_model.cluster_centers_)
```

The four cluster centers as predicted by our K-Means model has the following values

Output

```
[[48.26       56.48      ]
 [86.53846154 82.12820513]
 [87.        18.63157895]
 [26.30434783 20.91304348]]
```

In addition to finding cluster centers, the `K-Means` class also assigns a cluster label to each data point. The cluster labels are numbers that basically serve as cluster id. For instance, in the case of four clusters, the cluster ids are 0,1,2,3.

To print the cluster ids for all the labels, you can use the `labels_` attribute of the `K-Means` class, as shown below.

Script 12:

```
#printing predicted label values
print(km_model.labels_)
```

Output

```
[3 0 3 0 3 0 3 0 3 0 3 0 3 0 3 0 3 0 3 0 3 0 3 0 3 0 3 0 3 0 3
 0 3 0 3 0 3 0 3 0 3 0 3 0 0 0 0 0 0 0 0 0 0 0 0 0 0
 0 0 0 0 0 0 0 0 0 0 0 0 0 0 0 0 0 0 0 0 0 0 0 0 0 0 0
 0 0 0 0 0 0 0 0 0 0 0 0 0 0 0 0 0 0 0 0 0 0 0 0 0 0 0
 0 0 0 0 0 1 2 1 2 1 2 1 2 1 2 1 2 1 2 1 2 1 2 1 2 1 2 1 2
 1 2 1 2 1 2 1 2 1 2 1 2 1 2 1 2 1 2 1 2 1 2 1 2 1 2 1 2 1
 2 1 2 1 2 1 2 1 2 1 2 1 2 1 2 1 2 1 2 1 2 1 2 1 1]
```

The following script prints the clusters in different colors along with the cluster centers as black data points, as shown below.

Script 13:

```
#pring the data points
plt.scatter(dataset.values[:,0], dataset.values[:,1], c=
km_model.labels_, cmap='rainbow')


#print the centroids
plt.scatter(km_model.cluster_centers_[:, 0], km_model.
cluster_centers_[:, 1], s=100, c='black')
```

Output:

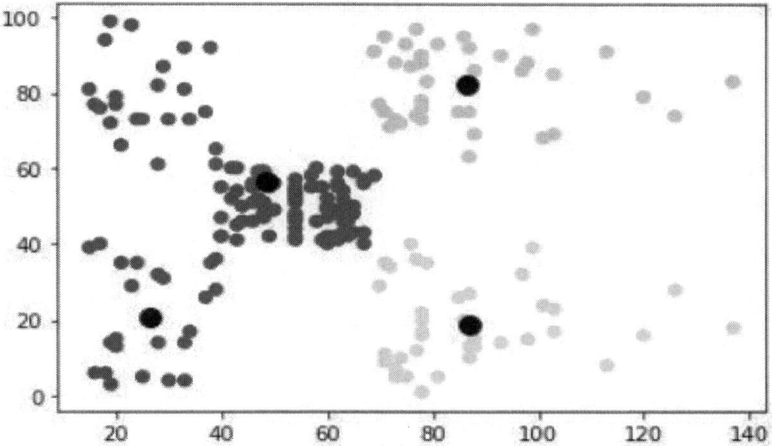

Till now in this project, we have been randomly initializing the value of K or the number of clusters. However, we do not know exactly how many segments of customers are there in our dataset. To find the optimal number of customer segments, we need to find the optimal number of K because K defines the number of clusters.

There is a way to find the ideal number of clusters. The method is known as the `elbow method.`

10.6. Elbow Method for Finding K Value

In the elbow method, the value of inertia obtained by training K-Means clusters with different number of K is plotted on a graph.

The inertia represents the total distance between the data points within a cluster. Smaller inertia means that the predicted clusters are robust and close to the actual clusters.

To calculate the inertia value, you can use the inertia_ attribute of the `K-Means` class object. The following script creates inertial values for K=1 to 10 and the plots in the form.

Script 14:

```
# training KMeans on K values from 1 to 10
loss =[]
for i in range(1, 11):
    km = KMeans(n_clusters = i).fit(dataset)
    loss.append(km.inertia_)

#printing loss against number of clusters

import matplotlib.pyplot as plt
plt.plot(range(1, 11), loss)
plt.title('Finding Optimal Clusters via Elbow Method')
plt.xlabel('Number of Clusters')
plt.ylabel('loss')
plt.show()
```

From the output below, it can be seen that the value of inertia didn't decrease much after five clusters.

Output:

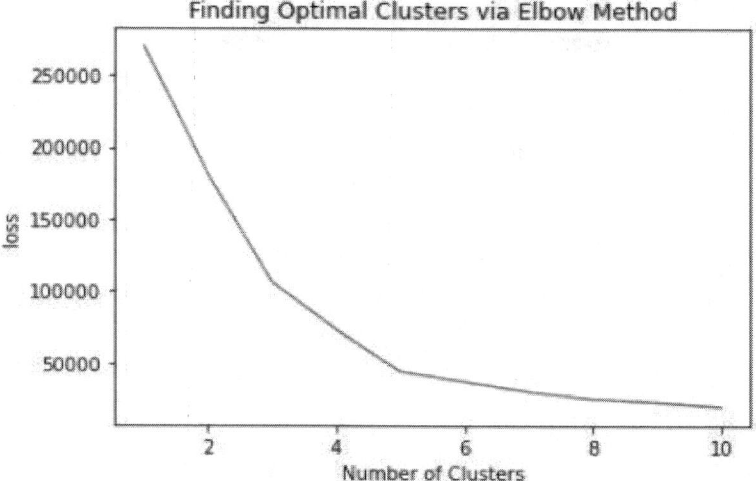

Let's now segment our customer data into five groups by creating five clusters.

Script 15:

```
# performing kmeans clustering using KMeans class
km_model = KMeans(n_clusters=5)
km_model.fit(dataset)
```

Output

```
KMeans(n_clusters=5)
```

Script 16:

```
#pring the data points
plt.scatter(dataset.values[:,0], dataset.values[:,1], c=
km_model.labels_, cmap='rainbow')


#print the centroids
plt.scatter(km_model.cluster_centers_[:, 0], km_model.
cluster_centers_[:, 1], s=100, c='black')
```

When K is 5, the clusters predicted by the K-Means clustering algorithm are as follows:

Output:

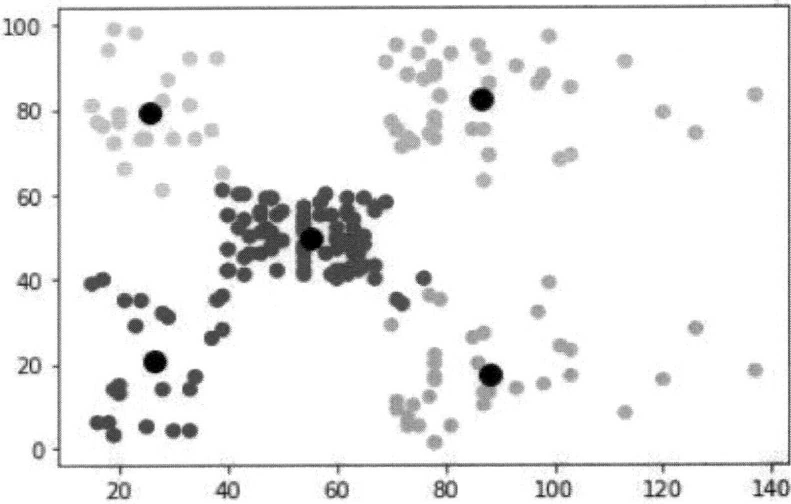

From the above output, you can see that the customers are divided into five segments. The customers in the middle of the plot (in purple) are the customers with an average income and average spending. The customers belonging to the red cluster are the ones with a low income and low spending. You need to target the customers who belong to the top right cluster (sky blue). These are the customers with high incomes and high spending in the past, and they are more likely to spend in the future, as well. So any new marketing campaigns or advertisements should be directed at these customers.

10.7. Finding Customers to Target for Marketing

The last step is to find the customers that belong to the sky blue cluster. To do so, we will first plot the centers of the clusters.

Script 17:

```
#printing centroid values
print(km_model.cluster_centers_)
```

Here is the output. From the output, it seems that the coordinates of the centroid for the top right cluster are 86.53 and 82.12. The centroid values are located at index 1, which is also the Id of the cluster.

Output

```
[[55.2962963  49.51851852]
 [86.53846154 82.12820513]
 [25.72727273 79.36363636]
 [88.2        17.11428571]
 [26.30434783 20.91304348]]
```

To fetch all the records from the cluster with id 1, we will first create a dataframe containing index values of all the records in the dataset and their corresponding cluster labels, as shown below.

Script 18:

```
cluster_map = pd.DataFrame()
cluster_map['data_index'] = dataset.index.values
cluster_map['cluster'] = km_model.labels_
cluster_map
```

Output:

	data_index	cluster
0	0	4
1	1	2
2	2	4
3	3	2
4	4	4
...	...	...
195	195	1
196	196	3
197	197	1
198	198	3
199	199	1

Next, we can simply filter all the records from the cluster_map dataframe, where the value of the *cluster* column is 1. Execute the following script to do so.

Script 19:

```
cluster_map = cluster_map[cluster_map.cluster==1]
cluster_map.head()
```

Here are the first five records that belong to cluster 1. These are the customers that have high incomes and high spending.

Output:

	data_index	cluster
123	123	1
125	125	1
127	127	1
129	129	1
131	131	1

Further Readings – Customer Segmentation

To study more about clustering for customer segmentation, look at these links:

https://bit.ly/3nqe9Fl

https://bit.ly/36EApVw

https://bit.ly/3nqhiW4

Exercise 10.1

Question 1:

Which of the following is a supervised machine learning algorithm?

A. K - Means Clustering
B. Hierarchical Clustering
C. All of the above
D. None of the above

Question 2:

In K-Means clustering, the inertia tells us?

A. the distance between the data points within a cluster
B. output labels for the data points
C. the number of clusters
D. None of the above

Question 3:

Which of the following are some of the disadvantages of K-Means clustering?

A. Manual selection of K value
B. Convergence depends upon the initial value of K
C. Outliers affect clustering
D. All of the above

From the Same Publisher

Python Machine Learning
https://bit.ly/3gcb2iG

Python Deep Learning
https://bit.ly/3gci9Ys

Python Data Visualization
https://bit.ly/3wXqDJI

Python for Data Analysis
https://bit.ly/3wPYEM2

Data Science with Python

https://bit.ly/3wVQ5iN

Statistics with Python

https://bit.ly/3z27KHt

Exercise Solutions

Chapter: Exercise 2.1

Question 1:

Which iteration should be used when you want to repeatedly execute a code specific number of times?

A. For Loop
B. While Loop
C. Both A & B
D. None of the above

Answer: A

Question 2:

What is the maximum number of values that a function can return in Python?

A. Single Value
B. Double Value
C. More than two values
D. None

Answer: C

Question 3:

Which of the following membership operators are supported by Python?

A. In

B. Out

C. Not In

D. Both A and C

Answer: D

Exercise 1.1

Question 1:

Which attribute of the LinearRegression class is used to print the linear regression coefficients of a trained algorithm:

A. reg_coef

B. coefficients

C. coef_

D. None of the Above

Answer: C

Question 2:

To make a prediction on a single data point, the data features should be in the form of a _______________:

A. column vector

B. row vector

C. row or column vector

D. scalar value

Answer: B

Question 3:

Which of the following is not a metric used to measure the performance of a regression algorithm?

A. Accuracy

B. Mean Absolute Error

C. Mean Squared Error

D. Root Mean Squared Error

Answer: A

Exercise 2.1

Question 1:

Which attribute of the TfidfVectorizer is used to define the minimum word count:

A. min_word

B. min_count

C. min_df

D. None of the Above

Answer: C

Question 2:

Which method of the MultinomialNB object is used to train the algorithm on the input data:

A. train()

B. fit()

C. predict()

D. train_data()

Answer: B

Question 3:

Spam email filtering with naive Bayes algorithm is a type of ______________ learning problem.

A. Supervised

B. Unsupervised

C. Reinforcement

D. Lazy

Answer: A

Exercise 3.1

Question 1 :

In a neural network with three input features, one hidden layer of five nodes, and an output layer with three possible values, what will be the dimensions of weight that connects the input to the hidden layer? Remember, the dimensions of the input data are (m,3), where m is the number of records.

A. [5,3]

B. [3,5]

C. [4,5]

D. [5,4]

Answer: B

Question 2:

Which of the following loss function can you use in case of a regression problem:

A. Sigmoid

B. Negative log likelihood

C. Mean Absolute Error

D. Softmax

Answer: C

Question 3:

Neural networks with hidden layers are capable of finding:

A. Linear Boundaries

B. Non-linear Boundaries

C. All of the above

D. None of the Above

Answer: C

Exercise 4.1

Question 1:

The shape of the feature set passed to the LSTM's input layer should be:

A. Number of Records, Features, Timesteps

B. Timesteps, Features, Number of Records

C. Features, Timesteps, Number of Records

D. Number of Records, Timesteps, Features

Answer: D

Question 2:

RNN is not capable of learning longer sequences because of:

A. Exploding Gradient
B. Diminishing Gradient
C. Low Gradient
D. None of the Above

Answer: B

Question 3:

An RNN is useful when the data is in the form of:

A. A table with unrelated records
B. An image with spatial information
C. A sequence with related records
D. None of the Above

Answer: C

Exercise 5.1

Question 1:

This process where the ground truth value of the previous output is fed as input to the next timestep is called teacher forcing.

A. Truth Labeling
B. Input Labeling
C. Input Forcing
D. Teacher Forcing

Answer: D

Question 2:

In the seq2seq model, the input to the node in the decoder layer is:

A. Hidden state from the encoder

B. Cell state from the encoder

C. A "start of sentence" tag

D. All of the above

Answer: D

Question 3:

To end predictions using decoder LSTM in seq2seq, what strategy is adopted?

A. End sentence if maximum sentence length is achieved

B. End sentence if "end of sentence" tag is predicted

C. Both A and B

D. None of the Above

Answer: C

Exercise 6.1

Question 1:

What should be the input shape of the input image to the convolutional neural network?

A. Width, Height

B. Height, Width

C. Channels, Width, Height

D. Width, Height, Channels

Answer: D

Question 2:

The pooling layer is used to pick correct features even if:

A. Image is inverted
B. Image is distorted
C. Image is compressed
D. All of the above

Answer: D

Question 3:

The ReLu activation function is used to introduce:

A. Linearity
B. Non-linearity
C. Quadraticity
D. None of the above

Answer: B

Exercise 7.1

Question 1:

What is the disadvantage of user-based collaborative filtering?

A. Users taste changes over time
B. More users than items
C. Complex and a higher number of computations
D. All of the Above

Answer: D

Question 2:

Which method is used to find the correlation between columns of two different Pandas dataframe?

A. get_corr()

B. corr()

C. corrwith()

D. None of the above()

Answer: C

Question 3:

Which method is used to find the correlation between the columns of a single dataframe?

A. get_corr()

B. corr()

C. corrwith()

D. corrself()

Answer: B

Exercise 8.1

Question 1:

To decrease the number of detections, the value of the minNeighbours attribute of OpenCV Cascade Classifiers should be:

A. Increased

B. Decreased

C. Kept constant

D. All of the Above

Answer: A

Question 2:

Which of the following is not a cascade classifier for face detection in Open CV?

A. haarcascade_frontalface_alt_tree.xml

B. haarcascade_frontalface_alt.xml

C. haarcascade_frontalface_default_tree.xml

D. haarcascade_frontalface_default.xml

Answer: C

Question 3:

To capture live video from the camera, which of the following values should be passed as an argument to cv2.VideoCapture() method?

A. 0

B. 1

C. 2

D. 3

Answer: A

Exercise 9.1

Question 1:

Dropout layer is added in a TensorFlow Keras neural network to:

A. Increase Accuracy

B. Reduce Overfitting

C. Reduce Loss

D. Increase Overfitting

Answer: B

Question 2:

In Keras Functional API, which of the following functions is used to add layers to a neural network model?

A. add()

B. append()

C. insert()

D. None of the above()

Answer: D

Question 3:

Which of the following functions can be used to add a new dimension to a numpy array?

A. add_dims()

B. append_dims()

C. expand_dims()

D. insert_dims()

Answer: C

Exercise 10.1

Question 1:

Which of the following is a supervised machine learning algorithm?

A. K - Means Clustering

B. Hierarchical Clustering

C. All of the above

D. None of the above

Answer: D

Question 2:

In K-Means clustering, the inertia tells us?

A. the distance between the data points within a cluster

B. output labels for the data points

C. the number of clusters

D. None of the above

Answer: C

Question 3:

Which of the following are some of the disadvantages of K-Means clustering?

A. Manual selection of K value

B. Convergence depends upon the initial value of K

C. Outliers affect clustering

D. All of the above

Answer: D

Made in the USA
Middletown, DE
04 March 2025